DIEULA M. PREVILON

DOES
GOD
SEE
ME?

*How God Meets Us
in the Center of Our
Trauma-Healing Journey*

A NavPress resource published in alli...
with Tyndale House Publishers

T0036112

NavPress.com

Does God See Me? How God Meets Us in the Center of Our Trauma-Healing Journey

Copyright © 2024 by Dieula Magalie Previlon. All rights reserved.

A NavPress resource published in alliance with Tyndale House Publishers

NavPress and the NavPress logo are registered trademarks of NavPress, The Navigators, Colorado Springs, CO. *Tyndale* is a registered trademark of Tyndale House Ministries. Absence of ® in connection with marks of NavPress or other parties does not indicate an absence of registration of those marks.

The Team:
David Zimmerman, Publisher; Deborah Sáenz Gonzalez, Editor; Olivia Eldredge, Operations Manager; Jennifer Phelps, Designer

Cover illustration of woman portrait by Jen Phelps. Copyright © 2024 by Tyndale House Ministries. All rights reserved.

Author photo copyright © 2023 by JCPenney. All rights reserved.

All Scripture quotations, unless otherwise indicated, are taken from the Holy Bible, *New International Version,*® *NIV.*® Copyright © 1973, 1978, 1984, 2011 by Biblica, Inc.® Used by permission. All rights reserved worldwide. Scripture quotations marked ESV are from The ESV® Bible (The Holy Bible, English Standard Version®), copyright © 2001 by Crossway, a publishing ministry of Good News Publishers. Used by permission. All rights reserved. Scripture quotations marked GW are taken from *GOD'S WORD*®. Copyright © 1995, 2003, 2013, 2014, 2019, 2020 by God's Word to the Nations Mission Society. Used by permission. Scripture quotations marked NIrV are taken from the Holy Bible, *New International Reader's Version,*® *NIrV.*® Copyright © 1995, 1996, 1998, 2014 by Biblica, Inc.® Used by permission. All rights reserved worldwide. Scripture quotations marked NLT are taken from the *Holy Bible,* New Living Translation, copyright © 1996, 2004, 2015 by Tyndale House Foundation. Used by permission of Tyndale House Publishers, Carol Stream, Illinois 60188. All rights reserved. Scripture quotations marked PAR are the author's paraphrase.

Published in association with Books & Such Literary Management, 52 Mission Circle, Suite 122, PMB 170, Santa Rosa, CA 95409-5370, www.booksandsuch.com

Some of the anecdotal illustrations in this book are true to life and are included with the permission of the persons involved. All other illustrations are composites of real situations, and any resemblance to people living or dead is purely coincidental.

For information about special discounts for bulk purchases, please contact Tyndale House Publishers at csresponse@tyndale.com, or call 1-855-277-9400.

ISBN 978-1-64158-755-6

Printed in the United States of America

30	29	28	27	26	25	24
7	6	5	4	3	2	1

We are living in a traumatizing world. The increased hostility, fear, and polarizing divisiveness weighs heavily on all of us. Using her years of experience, Dieula Previlon offers wise counsel and honest guidance to explore the question of whether we are loved, seen, and known by God. This timely book is an invitation to embark on a journey that leads to the joy of finding hope and healing from trauma that empowers women around the world to give birth to our truest selves. I highly recommend it!

DR. BRENDA SALTER McNEIL, author of *Becoming Brave: Finding the Courage to Pursue Racial Justice Now* and *Roadmap to Reconciliation 2.0: Moving Communities into Unity, Wholeness and Justice*

Dieula is brilliant, compassionate, and wise. She pastors, counsels, and coaches throughout her rich and practical book, *Does God See Me?*, ensuring that traumatized people experience Christ's freedom. I'll be recommending this book for years to come.

KAT ARMSTRONG, Bible teacher and author of *No More Holding Back*, *The In-Between Place*, and the Storyline Bible Studies

Black communities still engage the horrific belief that if you have Jesus, then you don't need therapy. Bucking such a belief, Previlon has produced a phenomenal workbook for Jesus-loving women who want to begin the healing journey from trauma while remaining connected to their spiritual and biblical roots. Kudos to Previlon for providing an accessible book that can help women on such a journey.

ANGELA N. PARKER, assistant professor of New Testament and Greek at McAfee School of Theology and author of *If God Still Breathes, Why Can't I? Black Lives Matter and Biblical Authority*

Dieula offers us a cherished dual gift of vulnerable experience and keen expertise within the pages of this book—and also gives us grounded hope. Through the lens of Hagar, an abused Egyptian whose captivity led her to the wilderness and likely death, Dieula teaches us what it is to be seen by God and to name God even after trauma. She bridges the gap between academic counseling concepts and everyday therapeutic practices, offering readers an accessible, embodied ethic of care. Like a true womanist, Dieula writes with the aim of gentle and expansive freedom for all of us, but especially for Black women, who have wrongly been presumed upon as the world's mules. God sees us as the beloved, and Dieula echoes this by showing us that trauma doesn't have the last word.

SHARIFA STEVENS, author of *Only Light Can Do That: 60 Days of MLK–Devotions for Kids* and contributor to *Vindicating the Vixens: Revisiting Sexualized, Vilified, and Marginalized Women of the Bible*

Does God See Me? is a well-crafted body of work that conveys an immense depth of vulnerability and hope for restoration. Dieula's personal life traumas and her journey toward healing are woven into a compelling narrative, and the book is full of practical restorative exercises, demonstrating her counseling expertise throughout. This book had a profound impact on me, and I strongly recommend that everyone buy a copy.

JENNIFER M. JOSEPH, pastor of Zion Community Church

Does God See Me? How God Meets Us in the Center of Our Trauma-Healing Journey is a much-needed read, especially now that *trauma* is becoming a household word. The opportunity for readers to do healing work in the comfort and privacy of their own sacred personal space is certainly a gift. This book offers solidly resourced practices and time-tested tools that have been gained through Dieula's professional experience in trauma-informed counseling. My best therapists have been the ones who have tapped into their own lived experience; like Dieula, they offered me the hope I needed.

JUANITA RASMUS, author of *Learning to Be: Finding Your Center after the Bottom Falls Out* for Sonny

Contents

Introduction *1*

PART ONE Understanding Your Trauma Story

1 Born into Trauma *11*

2 The God Who Sees You *25*

3 The Impacts of Trauma *37*

4 "Do You Want to Get Well?" *47*

PART TWO Facing Your Trauma Story

5 Grief *57*

6 Shame *71*

7 Domestic Violence *81*

8 Sexual Abuse *91*

9 Abandonment *103*

10 Racial Trauma *115*

PART THREE Finding Freedom from Your Trauma Story

11 Telling Your Story *131*

12 Lamenting Your Trauma Story *139*

13 Forgiving Others *147*

14 Forgiving Yourself *161*

15 Rediscovering Hope *171*

16 Embracing Joy *179*

Epilogue *189*

Acknowledgments *192*

Notes *196*

Introduction

Writing a book on trauma healing certainly exposed areas in my life I hadn't yet surrendered to the healing journey. I penned the first words of this book almost a decade ago, but the project stalled. I kept hoping that God would take away my desire to write about trauma healing and send someone more equipped to complete the book. I didn't consider myself a legitimate trauma expert with the professional knowledge that would qualify me to write about this topic. But perhaps this will serve as a witness that those of us who became experts through our own trauma stories can write books like this. The other expertise I can claim is sitting in the birthing room while many like you were going through the labor pains of birthing a new self from their trauma. I thank my clients for teaching me to not forgo being present and loving during those labor pains. Every day I'm learning new techniques to treat trauma and help victims reach a place of functioning and thriving.

A Life-Changing Trip to Kenya

My expertise in trauma began to grow long before I was counseling trauma survivors professionally. I have vivid memories of the trauma I witnessed and experienced growing up in Haiti and

America. Of course, in those formative years, I didn't have the language to classify these experiences as trauma. It wasn't until my late twenties that I became more aware and started asking questions. Why didn't we talk about certain topics in our family? Why did that relationship end in divorce? Why did this family leave the church? How about this secret relationship with so-and-so that we were never to speak of? How come everyone remained silent? How come no one stepped in? Why did so-and-so leave the family and become distant? The more I learned, the more my eyes were opened and the more questions I had. I was drawn to learning about trauma and how to approach the journey of recovery.

Spending time in several countries on the continent of Africa and in my native country of Haiti brought me great clarity. Years after graduating from Dallas Theological Seminary with a master's degree in counseling, I landed a job as the missions pastor at a megachurch in Dallas. While I was there, I led a mission trip to Mount Elgon in Kenya. It was my first trip to Africa. The training focused on helping women take steps toward healing from the unimaginable traumas they'd experienced during a postelection civil war. During the unrest, many of the women had seen their loved ones mutilated or sexually violated. There was terrible loss of life.

On the first day of the training program, the trauma was obvious to the trained eye. The women communicated minimally among themselves and crossed their arms. Their entire body language communicated *We are not here to make friends.*

Our team pressed on with the training and handed out the materials we had prepared. We didn't perform any miracles during those five days, but something clearly shifted in the women. Their body language began to communicate a different message. They were joyfully singing, clapping their hands, sitting with each other, and telling stories. They had moved to a place of freedom from their trauma.

That's when I knew I would dedicate my life to helping women recover from trauma. My life's work would be to offer this kind of freedom to women all over the world. Something inside me had shifted, too, and I mumbled a few private words in prayer: *In your grace, God, please allow me to be a part of this work.*

An Unexpected Ministry

Soon after that trip, I transitioned out of my role at the church. But things didn't go quite the way I had planned. There were no obvious opportunities at the time for me to help women find hope and healing from trauma. I felt as if that private moment with God in Africa had never happened! I went through a bout of depression with no vision, no hope, no income, no purpose, and no women to minister to. Or so I thought.

During that season of waiting, something inside me said, *There are women all over the world dealing with the impact of trauma in their lives. Find out where they are, and work with them.* It suddenly became quite clear that I should do two things: start a nonprofit organization—ElevateHer International Ministries—to help women heal from trauma, and volunteer in the women's unit at the Dallas jail.

I had ministered in Haiti a half dozen times, as well as in India and Kenya, but never in a million years did I think I'd be ministering to imprisoned women in my own city. I had always heard horror stories about the prison system—and violent, unruly people who had no respect for law and order. Though I was excited and willing to finally step into my calling, I was scared to death.

My first visit to the facility was anxiety producing. I parked in a neglected gravel lot across the street from the multistory, brown-bricked jail. Outside the facility were all kinds of people. People waiting on buses. People entering and leaving the facility. People who seemed to be just hanging around. Adults holding the hands of small children. Well-dressed people I assumed were visiting their loved ones. And a few homeless people who pitched their tents right outside the jail. I wondered about each of their stories and what had brought them to this place.

As I waited for the light to change so I could cross the street, I began to panic, wondering how in the world I had reached this point in my life. Part of me wanted to retreat to my car and forget about volunteering at the jail, but my tenacious spirit would never allow it. I could not back out of a commitment. Nothing would keep me from seeing those imprisoned women. Not even my fears. So I crossed the street and looked up at the two tall buildings in front of me. I couldn't believe those buildings were home to people our society considers the greatest sinners among us. Or that God was calling me to get to know them and sit with them through their trauma-healing journeys. But I walked into the jail and began the journey.

After my identification was processed and cleared, I joined two other women volunteers as we made our way to the women's wing. When the second steel door slammed shut behind us, I knew there was no turning back. (*Note:* If you're praying about being part of a prison ministry, get rid of any traces of claustrophobia, and don't watch any movies about prison before going!) We were buzzed into the room where we would be teaching for the night. Chairs were arranged in a circle, enough for twenty women. On both sides of the room were pods with glass doors. The women were completely exposed. I was trying hard not to stare, but I couldn't help it. Some were showering, some were using the toilet in their stalls, some were playing cards, some were watching TV, and others were in their bunks. I felt like I was on a mission trip in a different country, but I was only thirty minutes from my house.

One by one, the women walked into the room and took a seat.

They had puzzled looks on their faces as they waited to hear what I had come to offer them. I soon learned that they were excellent profilers. They could smell a con from a mile away. They could sense a manipulator with impure motives and could recognize those who truly came in the name of Jesus. It turns out that all of them had heard about Jesus, but they were waiting silently to see which Jesus I was representing: a condemning and judgmental Jesus or the Jesus who looked at them with compassion and love.

Our team's plan for the next six weeks was to study the lives of various women in the Bible and see if their stories resonated with the women at the Dallas jail. I named the study "Her Story, My Story, Our Story" and hoped the women would see a common thread in all our stories.

After introductions, I opened the night with a statement: "We all have a story to tell. What is your story?" Unlike many who interact with those in prison, I didn't want to talk as if I knew these women's stories, because I didn't. Only they knew how they'd arrived at this place in their lives. Without much coaxing, the women started to open up. As each one shared, I noticed that it was very hard for them to keep from crying. The pain in the room was palpable. At this point I realized the commonality between the women from Haiti, Kenya, and India and those in front of me. They were all humans created in the image of God with the capacity to be hurt deeply. As they shared their stories, I realized that most of their downward spirals had begun with someone abusing or violating them. Someone who was supposed to love them. My heart broke for these women. I felt compassion for them.

After that first night, I knew I was exactly where I needed to be, doing exactly what I was called to do: help women heal from trauma through the compelling story of Jesus, who has proven his love for women and who desires for them to flourish.

In jail, I became acquainted with women I never would have guessed would be in such a place. I met a woman working on her PhD and another woman who had once worked in a church. I even met a motivational speaker and writer. I quickly learned that trauma does not discriminate.

One night as I was teaching about the healing process and the common hindrances that hamper one's ability to dream, I noticed a new face in the group. This was a transient group of women who would often come and go. I might see a woman one week, and the next week she would either be paroled or just not show up. So it was common to see new faces at our meetings.

I was immediately drawn to this new woman. She had striking beauty, flawless skin, a warm smile, and hair arranged in perfectly braided cornrows. I immediately wanted to know her story. At that point, I'd learned enough about the women in jail to know not to ask about their stories right away. I had to earn their trust first, and once I had, I couldn't stop them from talking. As I continued to teach, she continued to listen without saying a word. The group would chime in and give feedback, but there was still not a word from her.

Then, after about thirty minutes of listening, she spoke up: "When I was little, I wanted to be an Olympic gold medalist in track and field." Her face lit up as she talked about the joy she felt when she ran. She had it all planned out in her mind; the gold medal was her dream. Then tears started streaming down her face as she told how life had taken a turn for the worse. "But when I was eight, my stepfather started sexually abusing me, and he kept abusing me until I was twelve. He threatened to kill my brother and mother if I ever told." This beautiful woman had attempted suicide several times, and one attempt had been quite severe.

This is the reality of trauma for many women. Trauma can involve a single event or a series of events that tear victims to pieces and leave them shattered. Without intervention, many are unable to function or put their lives back together. The problem with trauma is that it often doesn't end when the event has passed. Victims of trauma continue to experience it in their thoughts, emotions, and bodies. This woman who had dreamed of winning an Olympic gold medal had spent her entire life trying to escape the pain and suffering trauma had caused. And here she was in jail learning about the healing process. My heart felt her grief and the pain that hindered forward movement in her life. Again, it was in jail, hearing these women's stories, that I knew I had to be part of the healing process.

Jesus and Trauma Therapy

It was behind those prison walls that my trauma-healing ministry for women began. It was also behind those walls that the idea sprang to life for writing a book that centered on the trauma-healing journey. In that season, I started thinking about integrating therapeutic strategies and faith in Christ as a holistic model for trauma healing. Historically, the two have been at odds. The psychological world hasn't seemed too impressed with or interested in the value of spirituality in the healing journey. And in many religious circles where faith in Jesus is already central to one's life, the necessity of therapeutic resources has been called into question. But I believe that the integration of faith and therapeutics is necessary for healing. Like many others, I see great value in Jesus-and-therapy as a model for healing from trauma.

So I began this experiment with a question: What if we utilized therapeutic strategies and the principles Jesus taught to help imprisoned women begin taking steps toward healing from trauma? Week by week, the women would show up with their trauma stories, and our team would show up with Jesus and therapy. Week by week, we gave the women space to process their trauma through the Scriptures and therapeutic strategies. The more we leaned into that model, the more we began to see the impact it had on the women. Every week we'd see a release of emotions followed by confession and repentance. We witnessed truth telling, question asking, and feedback giving, and then we'd close in prayer. For two years, once a week, that model was our process. The women took steps toward healing, and God was present.

After working with the women in the Dallas jail, I became a licensed professional counselor (LPC) to increase my proficiency in trauma healing. I also took another step in my professional journey by embracing my calling as an ordained minister. I believe these shifts in my career were God's way of positioning me to partner with him. They also reinforced and reaffirmed my belief that the most effective model for trauma healing involves integrating good counseling strategies with a solid theological foundation rooted in the love of Christ. I have used this model of trauma healing and what I learned from the women in the Dallas jail to minister to women all over the United States, Kenya, Haiti, the Democratic Republic of the Congo (DRC), Brazil, and Uganda.

This book is for my sisters around the world who are ready to take their first steps toward healing from trauma. I invite you to join me on this healing journey. As we travel together, you will be reminded that God is not outside the healing process. He is at the center of it, fully present and walking with each of us every step of the way.

Our stories are important to him!

PART ONE

UNDER-STANDING YOUR TRAUMA STORY

1

BORN INTO TRAUMA

Misery won't touch you gentle. It always leaves its thumbprints on you; sometimes it leaves them for others to see, sometimes for nobody but you to know of.

EDWIDGE DANTICAT, *The Farming of Bones*

I was born into trauma. It has always been a presence in my life. The first story my parents ever told me, in fact, was a trauma story. As soon as I was born, I had to fight to survive. I became so ill that fear ripped through my parents and extended family. They even carved a coffin for my tiny body. My mother and other family members labored in prayer, moaning and crying and imploring God to preserve my life. To this day, I don't know what caused this illness.

At birth I was given the common Haitian name Magalie. But my father changed it to Dieula (pronounced "Jur-la"), which means "God is here" or "God is present" in Haitian Kreyol (or Creole). Because, as my mother tells the story, "if God wasn't present, you would've died." (If you took one look at Haiti's infant mortality rate, you'd know that giving birth there is often a traumatic event for women and their babies.) I'm still known as "Maga" to family and friends in our Haitian community, but Dieula is my official name—an avenue for sharing about God's saving grace.

During my childhood years, my three older sisters and I lived most of the year in the city with my aunt so we could attend quality schools and become, as they say, "civilized and educated" Haitians, thereby escaping the nation's pervasive poverty. In the city of Gonaïves, where I was born, the roads were paved, and some communities had electricity. Life was fast-paced, and there seemed to be businesswomen and men everywhere hawking their products. On my daily walk to school, I had to cross through the maché, an outdoor market that was open from sunup to sundown where you could find just about everything you needed.

I spent most of my summers in Haiti's countryside—andeyò in Kreyol—where my grandmother lived, and where some of my fondest memories were made. In the country, the pace of life was slower. Quality schools and education were rare. Resources weren't as plentiful, and the roads weren't paved, which didn't matter so much because people walked everywhere. At night, the sky was emblazoned with stars, unlike in the city. Andeyò was where Haiti's rice farmers lived and worked. I could roam freely there because everyone knew one another and looked out for each other's children. I would spend so many hours swimming in the lakes and canals and playing with my sisters, cousins, and kin that the sun would turn my dark hair a dusty brown. Everyone in the country was related in one way or another. There was a sense of peace and calm in rural Haiti that my soul still longs for.

Ti Anne

My grandmother was my favorite person in the world. She was a little woman in stature, but she was a powerhouse. An entrepreneur, she tended a small grocery store that sold items like Haitian rum, fruit soda, and rice. She was also a trusted leader and elder in the community who made sure that everyone had something to eat. Each day, she made sure that my sister and I delivered small plates of food to our neighbors.

Ti Anne—"Little Anne" in Kreyol—had a tenderness that was calming. If my sisters and I needed to be reprimanded, she would have a conversation with us, something completely unheard of in Haitian culture. Usually, any form of discipline required no explanation and would often be reactionary.

Gran Ti Anne was the first person in my life who made me feel loved and cared for. She doted on me and protected me. I felt safe with her. If anyone picked on me or made me sad for any reason, my grandmother would stand up for me and say, "Leave her alone! She wasn't nursed by her mother."

I remember first hearing these words when I was around four or five. I didn't fully understand what they meant at the time. Ti Anne was a source of comfort, so I knew she meant well, and this was her way of showing me love and protection. As an adult, I now recognize that she was talking about the trauma story surrounding my separation from my parents at a young age.

Just a few months after I was born, my mother and father left Haiti in search of a better life. They first landed on the Caribbean island of Saint Martin, then eventually made their way to the United States. Their lives as Haitian immigrants became such a survival ordeal that it kept them separated from their four daughters for ten years. I grew up knowing I had a mother and father, but I never experienced being mothered or fathered. Those years of separation left me with wounds—feelings of abandonment and missing out, of never knowing the tangible love of a mother or father in those vulnerable early years. Even now, these feelings resurface from time to time.

Leaving and Loss

As a child living in Haiti, I grew accustomed to hearing people talk about leaving. Everyone dreamed about finding a better life somewhere else. Some dreamed of leaving the country to live in the city; others dreamed of leaving their homes to live with family members who were better off than they were. And some, like my parents, dreamed of leaving Haiti altogether. We were all raised to understand and accept the sacrifices that families made for a better life.

Leaving, however, doesn't just involve the sacrifice and pain of children being separated from their parents. It comes with trauma. And from this trauma are birthed additional traumas.

I remember visiting my grandmother in the city hospital when I was seven or eight. I didn't know that it would be the last time I would see her alive. Then, suddenly, our trips to the country ceased. After Gran Ti Anne's death, I stopped thinking about andeyò. Perhaps a child's way of dealing with the trauma.

"When Grandma died," my sister recently told me, "there was no one left to take care of us [in the country], so we never went back."

The impact of trauma was multilayered. My sisters and I experienced loss upon loss upon loss. Though we were fortunate to have an aunt who cared for us, it wasn't the same as having a mother and father. Without my parents and my wise, protective grandma, I was vulnerable to sexual exposure, abuse, and even trafficking. I remember the men in our community exposing me to the male anatomy and destroying my childhood innocence. I know now that several adult men were grooming me for sex. I also remember the cousin who made sexual advances toward me. I recall as a nine-year-old looking for safe places to sleep when we visited my uncle. For many little girls in Haiti, the sexual exposure didn't stop at grooming. I've heard countless stories of young girls being sexually abused in circumstances like these, and my heart breaks for them. Every story of leaving Haiti or staying behind is marked by trauma.

Life in America

After a decade of being separated from our parents, my sisters and I joined them in America. Finally we were reunited. I know it sounds like a happy turn of events, but that wasn't the case for me because I was meeting my father and mother for the first time. These strangers carried a big piece of the puzzle of my existence and the key to my future, but I didn't know them at all.

I quickly realized that there were some obligations and expectations that went along with being part of a "family." I was supposed to feel connected to my parents because we shared DNA. And I felt a sense of indebtedness to them, as if I owed them loyalty without question. Therapeutically speaking, blind familial loyalty makes it difficult for people to heal from the trauma that occurs within the family. Without any explicit communication, I somehow knew that unconditional love was expected and should be reciprocated, even though there was no bonding or attachment between us to make that love real.

Though my parents had always planned to bring my sisters and me to America, it happened abruptly. There were no preparations or conversations about how difficult the transition from Haiti to America would be. And there were certainly no interventions from counselors, spiritual leaders, or wise elders. Nothing. The only thing that mattered was escaping from poverty.

I was supposed to be grateful for being delivered from a desperate situation in Haiti. I was supposed to understand that my parents had sacrificed a decade of their lives to provide this new life for my sisters and me. I wasn't allowed to question their decision or ask for anything else. We had finally stepped into our Canaan, a land flowing with milk and honey, the answer to all our problems. This new life demonstrated my parents' love, and so I created a compartment in my heart where I stuffed the trauma I experienced during this transition to the United States as a twelve-year-old Haitian immigrant. I never spoke a word about my pain to anyone until adulthood.

Navigating Life in a Strange New World

I remember my first day of school in New Jersey. Fifth grade with Mrs. Reid. Class had already started as I walked with a teacher's aide to the second-floor room. I still remember the terrible anxiety I felt that morning—flushed face, stomach in knots, and so faint I could've passed out or died. I didn't know to breathe, so I held my breath and hoped the moment would pass swiftly.

The moment I walked into class, the first order of business for Mrs. Reid and her students was figuring out how to pronounce my name, an issue I never had to deal with in Haiti. At the time, I didn't realize this would happen in every new classroom and with every new person I'd meet in America.

"What's your name?" Mrs. Reid asked.

I responded in Kreyol, "Dieula."

Mrs. Reid raised her voice and said, "Die-u-la?"

Again, I responded in Kreyol, "Non, Dieula."

Once again, she raised her voice and said, "Joola?"

Exasperated and flustered, I simply nodded oui, because by that time the entire classroom was listening to the conversation.

I often do this thing in my head where I rank the levels of trauma I've experienced. My grandma's death was at the top of my trauma scale, and my immigrant experience in America was probably second at that point. Someday I hope I will be able to just let my traumatic experiences be.

That season of my life brought deep feelings of loneliness. If death were an emotion, the loneliness I experienced was it. I went from being a gregarious preteen to being a mute. No one dared talk to the foreign girl, and that often made me happy, because I didn't possess the English words to respond. I hated lunchtime in the cafeteria, where I'd often find myself alone at a long lunch table. It felt as though a scorching spotlight were on me, exposing my pain and loneliness for all to see. To escape the pain, I would often skip lunch altogether and hide my twelve-year-old body behind a staircase. No one ever came to look for me. Proof of my invisibility came in the form of total isolation.

That season was also the genesis of my anxiety, something I'm still forced to manage today. Some days I would cry; other days I'd hold my breath, hoping no one would find me. I'd listen for voices and footsteps indicating when lunch ended so I could make my way to the playground. The playground proved difficult to navigate, but the other children were too busy running around or huddling with their friends to notice me, so I was relatively safe from their teasing. The playground also felt safer because of one particular lunch aide whose presence calmed my nerves. I stood close to her, knowing that nearness meant protection.

My ESL (English as a second language) teacher's presence also created a sense of safety for me. Ms. Canalas not only taught me how to speak English up through eighth grade; she helped in tangible ways as well. She even donated bags of clothes so my sisters and I could dress properly during the winter, since our Caribbean wardrobe wasn't up to the task.

But proximity to an adult didn't always ensure safety. In my tenth-grade English class, a group of boys made my life miserable. It seemed to be their purpose in life. One day stands out in my memory. To make sure I wouldn't be bullied, I waited until my older sisters had left for school, and then I dug through the closet we shared and grabbed one of my sister's nice blouses and wore it to school. I just knew that wearing this nice red blouse with puffy shoulders would finally end the teasing, bullying, and verbal abuse.

Boy was I wrong. Those bullies came up with ingenious new material to rip into me. I sat there weeping and frozen. My teacher watched, listened . . . and did nothing.

I found out that in America, unlike Haiti, the classroom was not safe for children like me. I often replayed the incident in my head, wondering why my teacher didn't use her authority to end the abuse. I've since realized that even the adults who are supposed to protect children from trauma don't always know what to do. I never dared express such pain to my family, of course, because we were immigrants. We did hard things well, or so the story goes. Already carrying the infamous label as the sensitive one in my family, I didn't want to let on that I wasn't doing well.

Suck it up, girl. Immigrants aren't weak. We're not supposed to feel pain when people throw insults at us. We're supposed to let it all roll off our backs—the epithets, the abuse, the trauma.

I'm reminded of the words of Edwidge Danticat in her book *The Farming of Bones*: "Misery won't touch you gentle. It always leaves its thumbprints on you; sometimes it leaves them for others to see, sometimes for nobody but you to know of."[1]

I remember hearing this saying when I first came to America: "I'm rubber, you're glue. Whatever you say bounces off me and sticks on you." Except I didn't find that to be true. All the insults stuck to me for a very long time.

"You look like a roach."

"You African booty scratcher."

"You don't belong."

"You're ugly."

"You're stupid."

"You speak with a stupid accent."

The reality is that many children dealing with trauma go unnoticed because they're often silent like I was, and quiet children are applauded for behaving well. Adults don't get close enough to create safe places for them to feel comfortable enough to share. At the time, I just knew that no one cared enough to rescue me.

My last year of high school ended with one more traumatic event that in some ways summed up everything I experienced during my adolescent years. By now I'd developed a disdain for school. It felt like a waste of time. Socially I had no hope of making friends, so I didn't even try. On this particular day after school, snow was on the ground, and my younger sister and I were eager to begin the two-mile journey home that we often walked together.

We exited the school from the side door and joined about half the students as we all parted ways for the day, each one with their own walking group. In front of the school, I innocently bumped into a girl I didn't know. I didn't think that would offend her, because we were all bumping into each other. She mumbled some words underneath her breath that I couldn't quite make out, and we both kept walking in opposite directions. But before I realized what was happening, I was face-to-face with this girl. She wrestled me to the ground, and her buddies joined her, punching and kicking me and pulling my hair. While I was on the ground getting hammered, with my sister doing her best to defend me, my only coherent thought was *Why me? What did I do to deserve this? Why is life always so hard for me?*

I often asked myself these questions, and for most of my life, there were no answers. Unanswered questions are one of the most frustrating aspects of the trauma-recovery process, because a part of me thinks that if I knew the answers and understood why, maybe it would hurt less. But answers don't always soothe the pain.

My immigrant church turned out to be my saving grace. It was the only place that came close to feeling safe for me to be seen. People spoke decently to me and seemed to accept me on some level. This community declared that my life mattered. When I felt the cruelty of the world, the church offered kindness. When the world made no sense, the church made sense. When people around me were unpredictable, the church modeled stability. The church helped me focus, and the loving support of this community ultimately propelled me to college.

On My Own

Rutgers University was a welcome change from the trauma of being an immigrant. By the time I entered college, my English had reached mastery level, and I'd become accustomed to America and its cultural differences. Finally, America started becoming enjoyable. College was the first time I slept in a bed I didn't have to share with anyone else. And I made some meaningful friendships with people who not only saw me but also made me feel like I belonged. Though the church had been a place of safety for me during those difficult adolescent years, it had also been a culture of rigidity that had told me I'd better stay in line or else. As a college student, I enjoyed the freedom of discovering new things beyond the gaze of my parents and the church.

College was fertile ground for my growth and development. But I also threw caution out the window. I met people from all over the world, and we'd compare stories and scars. Hearing their experiences started a healing process in me; I wasn't alone after all. I learned to have fun and not take life so seriously. Okay, if you want to know the truth, I partied like there was no tomorrow. I laughed like I'd just discovered laughter. For the first time, I was responsible for making life work. My parents couldn't support me beyond buying me a few outfits for college, so I got a part-time job. It felt great having control of my life. But having that control meant making mistakes I wasn't equipped to handle on my own.

While in college, I experienced another traumatic event: an unplanned, out-of-wedlock pregnancy. There were three things that made this event traumatic: my church, my parents, and my circumstances. My church operated by a strict set of rules, and anyone who broke them experienced rejection and shaming. That's how my church responded when I got pregnant outside of marriage. When my boyfriend and I decided to get married (since we loved each other), the church banished us to the basement to take our wedding vows. After we married, we weren't allowed to take Communion until after I gave birth. It was a punitive system, and while I believe it was done with the honor of the community in mind, the church made an example of us as a warning to other young, unmarried couples. It wasn't for the sake of God at all.

Then there were my parents. Every immigrant family comes to America to provide a better life for their children. I was the first to go to college in my family, and my parents were looking for proof that their sacrifices had paid off. So when I got pregnant, their pursuit of the American dream came to a screeching halt. The night I told my parents of my pregnancy, I didn't expect it to be the first and only time I saw my father cry. It tore me up to see their disappointment.

My circumstances at school pushed me to desperation. Living in a dorm and finishing my last semester, I had no job and no other place to live. No money, no savings. I just knew I couldn't go back home with a baby. Shame became a traveling companion. I felt that God was punishing me for having premarital sex. In fact, one person even commented that my morning sickness was a demonstration of God's judgment.

During that time in my life, everything felt painful emotionally and physically. Spiritually, I distanced myself from my church community because they kept emphasizing how God couldn't be in the presence of sin, which meant he couldn't possibly be with me, much less rejoice with me. I believed them. I created my own rigid categories for where God could and couldn't be, and one of the places he'd never dare to show up was in the life of a young, unmarried pregnant woman.

It would take years for me to realize that God doesn't require public penance for me to be right with him. Humans may have wanted to make sure I learned my lesson, to satisfy the cultural demand for bloodletting, but praise be to God for the blood of Christ that was shed for my sin. There is no need for further sacrifice. When the community behaves in ways that shame and punish, people fail to thrive, heal, and grow spiritually. I believe that loving, gracious, and forgiving communities promote human flourishing. Years later, I realized that God had more in store for me through this pregnancy than I or anyone else could ever have foreseen. I had just reached the starting point of my healing journey.

Almighty God, we thank you for being the God who can be found throughout our stories. You created us fearfully and wonderfully. Though we don't understand why we suffer, we know your purpose for us is not to harm us but to help us flourish. We pray that through this study, we will connect with you as the Suffering Servant, and we pray that because you are well acquainted with suffering, you will lead us on this healing journey. We ask you to restore the parts of us that have been broken and lost through trauma. Amen.

QUESTIONS TO EXPLORE

1. What attracted you to this book about healing from trauma?

2. Which parts of my story can you identify with?

3. My story has many pivotal moments. How did you feel as you read about the different layers of trauma I experienced?

4. What are some things you thought about God growing up that you later realized were false and not of God at all?

5. Make a list of the different emotions you felt reading my story. Where in your body did you feel those emotions?

FROM HEAD TO BODY

At the end of each chapter, I've included grounding exercises to help you engage your body in the trauma-healing journey. People who have experienced trauma often disconnect from their bodies out of a need for safety. They may be present physically but emotionally somewhere else. They essentially leave the present to cope with the overwhelming feelings of trauma.

The healing process requires grounding exercises to help you remain in the here and now while you work through what you experienced when the trauma took place. These grounding techniques can help you prepare for the healing journey. Here are some examples:

- Take a mental break and breathe deeply.
- Clap your hands.
- Stomp your feet.
- Take a short walk.
- Recite Scripture or poetry.

- Put your hand over your chest and feel your heartbeat.
- Rub your hands together or rub an object.
- Smell something soothing, like a candle or essential oils.
- Taste something sweet or sour.
- Name five things you can see, four objects you can feel, three sounds you can hear, two things you can smell, and one thing you can taste.

LET'S PRACTICE BREATHING

This book may bring up unpleasant memories at times, and you might find yourself out of breath. Breathing deeply will slow down the emotions. It will help calm your nerves, provide the oxygen your body needs, and keep you grounded and present.

- Take a deep breath from your nostrils for four seconds. As you breathe in slowly and deeply, you should feel your belly expanding.
- Hold your breath for four seconds.
- Then release it slowly for another four seconds.
- Then pause for another four seconds.
- Try this four times.

Use this breathing exercise whenever your emotions begin to feel unmanageable.

2

THE GOD
WHO SEES YOU

*[Hagar] gave this name to the LORD who spoke to
her: "You are the God who sees me," for she said,
"I have now seen the One who sees me."*

GENESIS 16:13

The other day, I unearthed an ancient VHS tape that turned out to be a video recording of my wedding. There I was, twenty-two and pregnant, hidden in the church basement with forty guests, a tiny number for a wedding in my community. Normally a Haitian wedding begins with a joyous procession of marching and dancing. But my husband and I were made to carry the weight of shame on our wedding day, so none of the customary celebrations ensued.

Denied the privilege of a white dress, I stood there in beige, a symbol of my unworthiness. Somehow, the emotions I had felt back then transferred to the present through this grainy video. One moment I was bravely smiling, and the next I was sobbing as an ambulance took away my husband, who had collapsed from a panic attack at the reception.

It almost sounds comical now, but I assure you it wasn't at the time. The video brought back so many negative memories, and I found myself crying for the younger me. She must have been so embarrassed knowing that everyone was scrutinizing her, assuming it was a shotgun marriage. Most of all, I remembered how numb I felt. I couldn't allow myself to enjoy that day.

After I mourned for what was, though, I couldn't help but reflect and marvel at today. That shamed woman is helping other women come out of their shame. The one who suffered humiliation is extending grace to others. Here I am in the role of a healer through my work as a pastor, counselor, and author. My trauma-healing journey has brought me to a place where I can direct others along the same path, holding on to God's hands as we walk together.

Hagar's Story

I'll never forget the day I was studying my Bible and met another young, desperate pregnant woman. Her name was Hagar. It was through her story that I first began to understand God's heart for the traumatized.

Hagar's story is found in Genesis 16. It is actually a story inside a story. We find her story tucked within the narrative of Abraham, the "father of faith," and his wife Sarah, who were called Abram and Sarai at the time. God revealed that he would give Abram and Sarai descendants more numerous than the stars in the sky (15:4-5). There was an enormous problem with that plan, however, because Abram was in his eighties, and Sarai was in her seventies. Sarai was also a barren woman who had never been able to conceive a child. So as they sometimes did in that culture, she gave her maidservant—an Egyptian slave named Hagar—to her husband so Hagar could conceive a child for them. That child would be considered theirs, like in the practice of surrogacy today.

This is where Hagar steps into the narrative. As I mentioned, she was a slave, a foreigner whom Abram likely acquired as a maidservant for Sarai. Hagar probably didn't speak the language of her master and mistress. And did I mention her gender? As a woman, a foreigner of a different race and ethnicity, and a slave, she was at the very bottom of the social hierarchy.

Not surprisingly, she did exactly as her masters told her to. Some Bible translations say that Abram "slept with Hagar" (16:4), but this wasn't some romantic scenario. Hagar had a duty to perform as a slave, and that duty was to birth a child. We also see some language in this chapter that has always puzzled me: "When [Hagar] knew she was pregnant, she began to despise her mistress. Then Sarai said to Abram, "You are responsible for the wrong I am suffering. I put my slave in your arms, and now that she knows she is pregnant, she despises me. May the LORD judge between you and me" (verses 4-5).

I find myself pausing at these two verses because I don't understand how a slave with no power had the right to explicitly despise her mistress. In her book *Womanist Midrash*, Wilda Gafney makes a poignant point that clarifies the matter: "It may not be that Hagar views Sarai as nothing because Sarai is infertile and Hagar is fertile. Rather, it may be that Hagar regards Sarai as nothing and/or curses her because Sarai uses Hagar's body for her own reproductive purposes. Why should a sex-slave, forced into gestating someone else's child, think highly of or bless her enslaver?"[1]

So Sarai became indignant with Abram and blamed him for Hagar's contempt, and Abram responded by putting the problem back on his wife. "Don't blame me," he said. "She's your slave—do with her as you wish" (verse 6, PAR).

Sarai seized those words and did as she pleased, abusing Hagar so harshly that the slave girl had no choice but to run away to save her life and the life of her unborn child. She fled into the desert and stopped near a spring, where she met an angel of the Lord God. The angel gave her hope, promising to make the child inside her womb into a great nation. Hagar then made a declaration many of us know well: "You are the God who sees me. . . . I have now seen the One who sees me" (verse 13).

Hagar's story is one of trauma on top of trauma. She was a dark-skinned, foreign, enslaved woman with no power or status. She was also the only person in the entire Bible who was given a voice and a platform to name God.

In the first part of verse 13, Hagar said, "You are El Roi, the God who sees me" (PAR). Her name for God tells me that she likely felt the way I did for many years and had a similar narrative playing in her head: *God doesn't see me or care for me.* But then she came to a turning point. When she ran into the desert to escape Sarai's abuse, she wasn't expecting God to show up. But he showed up supernaturally and provided life-sustaining water for her and her son to drink (Genesis 21:8-21). Hagar's story is for all of us who feel like God has forgotten us.

As I reflect on my own story of trauma and recovery, Hagar's story reminds me that God is present in the center of our trauma. He saw me, and he sees you. He knows our names, and he will not leave any of his children's stories without a redemptive ending. When I was going through my seasons of trauma, God felt distant. He did not seem present. Many days and months I lamented that God must not see or care for Black women like me, because the worst always seems to fall on us.

Similarly, I never thought God would show up supernaturally, as he did in Hagar's life, and provide me with life-sustaining nourishment. He provided the comfort of a grandmother who loved me deeply. He showed me that he cared through an ESL teacher who paid attention to my needs. He protected me through a lunch aide whose nearness offered comfort. He provided a church community that made me feel like I belonged when I was young and new to the US. He showed up through college mentors who broke bread with me and listened to my stories. He gave me lifelong friends who remind me I'm not alone. He provided counselors, spiritual directors, pastors, and life coaches who helped me walk through each step of the healing process. He saw me and took my hand and provided all the healing I needed.

Hagar's name for God tells me that he sees all of us in our afflictions, especially those who feel as if they're invisible and have no voice.

- For those crossing a dangerous border in search of life, God sees you.
- For those who've dealt with unspeakable traumas, God sees you.
- For those who've dealt with loss after loss, God sees you.
- For those who feel as if they're at the bottom of society's ladder, God sees you.
- For those who live in poverty and have never tasted the fruits of material wealth, God sees you.
- For those who keep going to a dried-up well for life-sustaining water, God sees you.
- For those who are suffering alone, God sees you.
- God sees you and knows your name.

The second part of verse 13 introduces the language of healing: "I have now seen the One who sees me."

During Hagar's conversation with God, her eyes were opened. This is the same process of regeneration and restoration that the woman at the well in John 4 experienced. For the first time, she was able to see the God who saw her.

That's my prayer for this book: that you might have eyes to see the God who sees you and take steps toward the healing he offers. That you might be awakened to the presence of God in your life every single day and know that you are not walking all alone.

As we walk together through this trauma-healing journey, I pray that you will enter into *mutual* seeing: that you will see the One who sees you.

A Savior Who Understands Our Trauma

Because God saw the pain and suffering I walked through, he provided the help, support, healing, and deliverance I needed. And he will provide complete healing when Christ returns. I can always rely on a Savior who identifies directly with the pain of the traumatized. Jesus left his throne of power and privilege in heaven, reestablished his presence with those he had created, and walked among them. He didn't roll into town in a gold-plated chariot wearing fancy threads; he walked right into the messiness of a persecuted minority group—the Jews—living as they lived, hurting as they hurt, making their trauma his own, grieving as they did, and dying as they would. Then he rose from the dead, proving to them and us that there is life after death and that he controls this life that is to come after death.

Thanks be to God that our Savior understands trauma. Our Savior understands when we lament, *God, you don't see me, and you don't care*. In the depths of his trauma, this Savior cried out similar words of lament: "My God, my God, why have you forsaken me?" (Matthew 27:46). And because pain and suffering unite us more than anything else, I know I can trust the authenticity of his pain. I can also trust his resurrection, this new life that conquered death. When he presents a path toward healing, toward eating the bread of life, toward drinking living water for sustenance, I can take him up on that proposal to heal, to eat, to drink, to be nourished. To experience freedom and new life through him.

Will you eat, drink, and be nourished so you can experience this freedom and new life?

As I was working on this chapter, I met with a young woman who sought me out for counseling help. She was in her last year of college but found herself with an unexpected pregnancy. I was instantly reminded of my own experience and the trauma that an unplanned pregnancy can cause for a woman—feeling lost, confused, and ashamed, knowing that the child inside will change the trajectory of her life forever. My pregnancy did, in fact, change the trajectory of my life. God used the birth of my son to turn my life around. It was at this juncture that Christ met me and began taking me on a journey. It was my "well experience" with God, like that of the Samaritan woman in John 4. It was my spring in the desert, like in the story of Hagar. It was at that moment I began to see the God who sees me. It was the genesis of my calling: to be a voice that preaches the good news of Jesus Christ and an instrument of healing in the lives of other women who experienced trauma. This was a moment for rejoicing, not for shaming and doling out punishment.

I use the word *journey* or *process* to describe the healing of traumatic wounds, because that's exactly what it is. Accepting the offer to heal doesn't mean you will wake up healed the next day. What it does mean is that each day, you accept the transformation that occurs when you fight and choose life, when you choose healing, when you choose freedom.

As we move into this healing journey, I invite you to commune with God at the Lord's Table. I pray that this book will help you eat and drink with him in a way that radically transforms your healing journey.

> *Lord Jesus Christ, we come to this sacred table not because we must but because we may. We come to testify not that we are righteous but that we sincerely love you and desire to be true disciples. We come not because we are strong but because we are weak. We come not because we have any claim on the grace of God but because in our frailty and sin, we stand in constant need of your mercy and help. We come not to express an opinion but to seek your presence and pray for the Spirit. Lord, be our guide. Amen.*

God and Trauma Healing

At this point, you might be wondering, *Could God actually bring about healing from the trauma I've experienced?*

My response is simple: Yes, I believe he can. Because I've found healing from the trauma I suffered, I know this to be true: There is a God, he is good, he loves us, and his desire is for our flourishing. I believe that the Bible, when studied contextually, historically, and responsibly, brings about healing and freedom for all people. I believe that the God we read about in the Bible is a living God who continually pursues us, is for us, and has the power to heal us from physical, emotional, and spiritual wounds as we trust in his Son, Jesus.

A huge part of Jesus' ministry on earth was to heal and give new life. In John 10:10, Jesus said, "The thief comes only to steal and kill and destroy. I came that they may have life and have it abundantly" (ESV). Jesus is confident in his power to bring about new life for those who accept his invitation to walk with him on the healing journey. The journey of trauma healing goes much deeper when we take Jesus with us. I believe it, I've experienced it, and I desire for you to experience healing, restoration, and freedom so you can flourish too.

Tools and Tips for the Journey

Before we continue this healing journey, there are some key tools I recommend to help you position yourself for transformation.

- *Intentionality.* Any process that's worth the effort must be entered intentionally. It is vital to be intentional about beginning the journey of healing. Reading this book on autopilot will not produce the transformation you're seeking. It is important that you take that first step intentionally and then many more to keep progressing. It is also important to remember that the journey of healing is not a sprint; it's a marathon. It will not be completed overnight. But with each small step, you'll move closer to a different and better you.

- *Time with God.* Throughout my journey, I've taken note of the atmosphere that best allows me to hear and respond to God. Some of the most profound experiences I've had with him have been in nature. I encourage you to pay attention to how you best connect with God and then honor those pathways. It could be walking in the park. Spending time in silence. Watching children play. Reading Scripture. Praying. Reflecting with a friend. These will probably be the times you hear from him the most sweetly and clearly.

- *Journaling.* In sixth grade, during one of the most challenging seasons of my life as my family was transitioning to America, my teacher gave me something that changed my life: a journal. Every day after recess, she'd give her students time to pause and write down our thoughts and feelings.

That simple act was one of the best things that happened to me. I've been writing in journals ever since. Journaling can be a tool to help you process thoughts, reflections, poems, prayers, and conversations with God. It's your private space to record the different things your brain is desperately trying to make sense of. What you write in your journal doesn't have to make sense to anyone but you. Your journal is a traveling companion of sorts. It will also document your progress through the trauma-healing journey.

• *Perseverance and Patience.* Sometimes the journey of healing from trauma feels like two steps forward and three steps back. It can be discouraging to see how slowly progress can move. It might even feel as if there's no end in sight and that the intense emotions the process stirs up will trouble you forever. Yet it's important to stay the course, give grace to yourself, and be patient. Every day, commit to putting one foot in front of the other and continuing the journey.

• *Self-Care.* Self-care is about learning to listen to your needs and honor them. It is not selfish to want to care for yourself. Without good self-care practices, you won't have the emotional stamina to complete the healing journey. Taking time for self-care demonstrates love for yourself and respect for the healing process. So whether it's sleeping in, watching a favorite show without guilt, going for a long walk, dancing, singing, clapping, breathing deeply, meditating, practicing mindfulness, enjoying yoga, gardening, exercising, crocheting, painting, coloring, listening to music, training for a marathon, or spending time with friends, self-care is extremely important. Listen to your body, and you'll know how to care for yourself.

- *Community Support.* Throughout my healing journey, I've realized that meaningful change and healing rarely take place outside a supportive and loving community. These are your cheerleaders—people who love you unconditionally, see you as you are, and still want to stick around. People you have given permission to speak into your life. Those who support you without tuning out when they're weary. Those whose words are soothing. Those who can tell you the truth (while being loving and gracious), which helps move you forward. Those who pray for you and are committed to seeing you through the journey.

- *Professional Counselors, Spiritual Directors, Life Coaches.* This book isn't intended to replace professional help. It should be used as a supplemental resource to help you along your healing journey. Pay attention to your emotional needs as you dive into this book and assess whether professional help is necessary. It's important to reach out for professional help if you have uncontrollable anxiety, depression, or any reactions that feel too difficult to handle alone for an extended period of time.

Father, please take each of us by the hand and lead us in this journey of healing. Provide us with everything we need for healing to take place. You know our needs intimately, better than we do. So lead us and guide us. Give us willing hearts so we can trust you in this process. Show up in the areas that this study can't. Please give us eyes to see the God who sees us. In Jesus' name, amen.

QUESTIONS TO EXPLORE

1. What was your response when you read Hagar's story? What do you think about the name she gave to the Lord?

2. What thoughts and feelings are you aware of when you consider that the creator of the universe sees you?

3. Which of the tools we discussed do you think will be most helpful to you as you begin your healing journey?

4. Which self-care practices will you use?

FROM HEAD TO BODY

Every last one of us has a place where we feel safe, at home, fully accepted, and at peace. You might have been to that place before or hope to go there one day. Imagine being there right now. Describe it. What do you see, feel, and hear? What smells are around you? Stay in that place for a minute and bask in it.

Now pay attention to your body. How does each part feel? Your face? Your throat? Your shoulders? Your chest? Your stomach? Your legs? Allow yourself to feel whatever this place makes you feel. And take some deep breaths. Stay there for five minutes or however long you can handle.

When painful memories are triggered on this journey, I want you to pause, close the book, take a break, and go back to that place. Ground yourself. This is your safe space, where you'll feel at home, fully accepted and at peace. Give it a try and allow yourself to feel safe again.

3

THE IMPACTS
OF TRAUMA

*The way we like to think about trauma in the somatic
literature is this notion of too much, too fast, too soon. When
our body is overwhelmed by much stimulation, by too much
external distress, if it feels like it's coming at us too fast, or
if it comes at us before we're prepared for it and our system
is not ready for it, that creates a traumatic situation.*

ALBERT WONG,
Somatic Approaches to Healing Trauma

In 2010, I began to focus more intentionally on serving the traumatized through my work with the women of Haiti. My first trauma conference in Haiti was right after the 7.0-magnitude earthquake that took an estimated three hundred thousand lives. I joined a group of US clinicians and other professionals to offer training and support for women who were suffering from post-earthquake trauma. But the conference ended up being so much more.

Once we taught the women about trauma and gave them the language to process it, we separated them into small groups so they could share their experiences. Then something amazing happened: More traumatic stories started coming out, but they had nothing to do with the earthquake. This conference reaffirmed that teaching women about trauma and its characteristics can be a powerful tool in the healing process.

One look at this world, and we can see that something's wrong, something's off, something's broken. We are not okay. We can feel it and sense it in our bodies. Trauma of all kinds reminds us that the world is not how it should be. In my journey as a trauma-healing professional, the question "Why do bad things happen to good people?" often comes up. We're constantly trying to understand the why behind trauma. The answer I often point to is sin. The biggest impact sin has had on us is destroying relationships of all kinds—relationships with God, ourselves, others, and even the earth.

Characteristics of Trauma

If you've experienced any type of trauma, you likely have a pretty good idea of what it is, but I want to take a moment to discuss the technical aspects and characteristics of trauma.

As we learned in the introduction, trauma is an event, or a series of events, that is so distressing, it tears its victims to pieces and leaves them shattered. The reality is that trauma doesn't simply end when the event does. Our brains and bodies continue to experience it. It's like a nightmare that never ends. Without intervention, we don't wake up.

The *Diagnostic and Statistical Manual of Mental Disorders (DSM)*, a handbook for mental-health and health-care professionals in the United States, describes a traumatized person as someone who has had "exposure to actual or threatened death, serious injury, or sexual violence in one of the following ways: (1) directly experiencing the traumatic events(s); (2) witnessing, in person, the event(s) as it occurred to others; (3) learning that the traumatic event(s) occurred to a close family member or close friend . . . ; or (4) experiencing repeated or extreme exposure to aversive details of the traumatic event(s)."[1]

Trauma is a threat that leaves you feeling like you or a loved one may die or be seriously injured. That kind of threat causes your body to shift automatically into an autopilot protective mode that engages a fight, flight, or freeze survival response. Once you survive a traumatic event, you may experience any of the following issues, which can develop over time into post-traumatic stress disorder (PTSD):

- reliving the trauma
- having sudden, lifelike memories called *flashbacks*
- having nightmares
- feeling disconnected from family and friends
- feeling that you won't live very long
- feeling depressed
- losing interest in the things you once enjoyed
- finding it difficult to sleep
- getting angry easily
- being unable to concentrate
- being startled easily
- being very aware of little sounds or movements
- having panic attacks
- experiencing physical pain
- having a strong response to things that remind you of the trauma
- trying hard to avoid thoughts, feelings, conversations, places, or people that remind you of the trauma
- struggling with addiction

Gabor Maté had this to say about addiction, one of the most common reactions to trauma:

> Addiction is not a choice that anybody makes; it's not a moral failure; it's not an ethical lapse; it's not a weakness of character; it's not a failure of will, which is how our society depicts addiction. Nor is it an inherited brain disease, which is how our medical tendency is to see it. What it actually is, is a response to human suffering, and all these people that I worked with had been serially traumatized as children. All the women had been sexually abused. All the men had been traumatized, some of them sexually, physically, emotionally neglected. And not only is that my perspective, it's also what the scientific and research literature show. So, addiction then . . . rather than being a disease as such or a human choice . . . it's an attempt to escape suffering temporarily.[2]

Our individual responses to trauma will not all look the same, but all of them are our "attempt[s] to escape suffering."

Many people who have experienced trauma may remain in fight, flight, or freeze mode even after the event has passed, if there is no awareness or intervention. It's as if the person continues to fight a threat that is no longer present. This is one of the reasons recovery is vital. The implications for thriving, not just surviving, are enormous.

The Importance of Awareness and Healing

We're all on a journey toward healing and restoration. From the moment original sin opened the eyes of Adam and Eve to a new reality, trauma, pain, and suffering have been part of the human experience. (These events are recorded in Genesis 3.) At some point in this life, most of us will encounter some kind of pain that will threaten to destroy our lives. And if we aren't aware and intentional about entering the journey of healing and restoration, it very well could.

Awareness of How Trauma Is Impacting You

To enter the trauma-healing journey, each of us must be aware of the impact trauma has had on our lives. Carrying trauma is costly, and it can impact us in many ways. Trauma can wreak havoc on our physical bodies, causing illness and pain that ultimately age us. It can also stunt us emotionally, socially, and spiritually and lock us in cycles of destruction. Trauma can leave us bitter, angry, and resentful if we allow it to. And it can cause crippling fears and anxiety.

The lingering effects of past trauma can keep us fighting a threat that is no longer present. It can leave us feeling bound, enslaved, and imprisoned in our minds, unable to move forward in life.

Trauma can also severely affect our relationships, romantic or otherwise. We can feel unable to be fully genuine and authentic in our relationships because our guard is always up. We may also be cautious and distrusting of others. These reactions disconnect us from others and keep us from enjoying meaningful relationships.

Trauma also impacts the way we function in the world. It can control every move we make in our lives—where we go, the types of relationships we engage in, and even the careers we pursue. It can stifle us, holding us back from doing bigger and better things in life. It can keep us from venturing out of our comfort zones and pursuing our dreams. Trauma often distorts our view of the world, so that instead of seeing all the beauty God has created, we believe that everyone is out to get us. When we expect only bad things to happen in our lives, we can miss out on so many good things, including miracles.

The healing process can feel daunting because it requires us to reenter our pain, process it, and create a new narrative for our lives. I completely understand why many choose not to enter this process. But there's no other way. As one old saying goes, "It feels worse before it can feel better." This is often the case in emotional healing.

The Healing Process

I am often reminded that healing is necessary because we have a mission that can only be accomplished on the other side of pain— or at the very least, with an awareness of how the pain is impacting our lives. When a person has experienced healing from trauma, you can physically see the difference. The women we ministered to in Kenya experienced that kind of healing. The difference in their lives was like night and day.

Not long ago, while I was walking in the park, I fell on the concrete, bruising both knees and slightly twisting my ankle. Not only was it embarrassing and painful, but it also took several weeks for my injuries to heal. According to Merriam-Webster's online dictionary, the word *heal* literally means "to make sound or whole."[3] It's amazing how our bodies can heal themselves and restore wholeness, but the process takes time.

There are three key aspects of physical healing that I want to focus on: repair, replacement, and regeneration. In an article on tissue repair,[4] the word *repair* is defined as "the restoration of tissue architecture and function after an injury." *Replacement* takes place when "severely damaged or non-regenerable tissues are repaired by the laying down of connective tissue, a process commonly referred to as scarring." And *regeneration* is "a type of healing in which new growth completely restores portions of damaged tissue to their normal state."[4]

The process of physical healing applies to our emotional-healing journeys. Once we gain an awareness of what trauma is and how it impacts our lives, we must enter the process of repair, replacement, and regeneration so that emotional healing can take place.

First, we need to repair the damage that trauma has caused by mending the broken parts of our lives. Next, we need to replace old patterns and negative thoughts with new ones. These old and toxic thoughts, patterns, and narratives cause even more emotional pain, but new thoughts, strategies, and narratives can set us free.

The final step in the healing process is regeneration, or rebirth. The concept of regeneration is demonstrated throughout the New Testament. For example, the Samaritan woman who spoke with Jesus at the well experienced a shift or rebirth of sorts that caused her to run out to tell everyone about Jesus: "[He] told me everything I ever did" (John 4:29).

Anyone who is suffering from trauma can find new life through Jesus Christ and be awakened to a new reality, a new identity as a new creation in Christ (2 Corinthians 5:17), and a new path that leads to life. I have experienced that process of regeneration, and you can too.

Trauma and its painful aftermath do not have to have the final word in your life. Your past trauma can propel you toward a greater purpose as you follow the path of healing. Healing is necessary for your growth and for living out your calling on this earth. Awareness of trauma and its impact is key in this process. But even more important is intentionality. Be intentional each day about pursuing the healing that God has for you.

Deuteronomy 30:19 says, "I have set before you life and death, blessings and curses. Now choose life, so that you and your children may live."

Let's keep walking this healing journey together so that we may truly live. The healing you experience will create ripple effects that will impact not only your life but also the lives of those closest to you—and generations to come.

Most gracious God, we come to you by the power of the Holy Spirit through Jesus' sacrifice on the cross, and we stand in victory because of his resurrection. We boldly come to you not because we have made all the right decisions and lived perfectly according to your ways but because you love us more than we can understand, more than we love ourselves. It is because of that love we are given second, third, and two thousandth chances. We thank you this day for giving us yet another chance to heal and become all that you have called us to be. Right now we pray that you will prepare our hearts, minds, and souls for the healing process. In your mercy, love, and grace, guide us through these weeks as we step into a new phase of healing. In Jesus' name we pray, amen.

QUESTIONS TO EXPLORE

1. What is one new thing you've learned about trauma from our discussion? Write down anything that has resonated with you.

2. How has trauma impacted your body, your relationships, and the way you navigate in the world? Has a lack of healing kept you from pursuing or accomplishing something?

3. In your journal, draw a picture that represents what it feels like to carry the weight of unhealed trauma. Describe your picture to a friend, your therapist, or your group. Then draw a picture showing what a healed person looks like. Describe your picture.

4. What does healing mean to you? Use one word to describe where you are in the healing process. Write a brief explanation for choosing that word.

5. Through Christ Jesus we can experience new life, healing, and freedom to accomplish his purposes for us. What does this mean to you?

FROM HEAD TO BODY

Being stuck emotionally and unable to move forward in your healing journey can show up in your body. Sometimes, the body can go places the mind is unprepared to enter. The following exercise is a gift from the women of the Democratic Republic of the Congo, where our team conducted trauma training. Following a break, I noticed that one of the Congolese leaders was guiding the women in a physical exercise to release tension in their bodies. In the US, this exercise is sometimes called a *body scan* or *progressive muscle relaxation*, but the DRC women added depth that I had never seen before. They also reminded me that they had everything they needed to aid them in their trauma-healing journeys.

So join the women of the DRC in a deep body scan.

- Get comfortable in a seated position or even standing. Close your eyes or keep them open. Whatever makes you most comfortable.

- Start with your lower body. Observe how your feet feel on the ground. Gradually move your focus to your ankles, knees, thighs, and pelvis. Pay attention to temperature, pressure, tension, and any other sensations as you move up your body.

- When or if you feel any tightness, take a deep breath and then exhale as you release it. When you sense the body part relax, you can move to the next one.

- When you have finished with the lower part of your body, do the same with your upper body. You may even include some of your internal organs, such as your stomach, heart, and lungs. The women in the DRC included their breasts and underarms.

- Finally, focus on your neck, face, and head. Your whole body should feel relaxed by the end of the exercise. Take note of any feelings or thoughts you have in this state.

4

"DO YOU WANT TO GET WELL?"

When Jesus saw [the disabled man] lying there and
learned that he had been in this condition for a long
time, he asked him, "Do you want to get well?"

JOHN 5:6

Toward the end of January 2020, I was on a plane heading to Uganda for a trauma-healing conference where I would be teaching a group of South Sudanese women refugees who were living in the city of Kampala. This was the first time I was on a trip doing what I loved while reeling from my own trauma and grief. I will share more about this traumatic experience later, in another chapter. This training ministry had been planned months before, but I knew that being in the company of other grieving women would be difficult. A part of me wanted to physically leave the US in the hope that leaving would lessen my grief. Africa has always been a special place for me because it ushered me into a different space for healing to take place. But that season of trauma had me feeling empty and broken. I had never felt that kind of brokenness during my adult life. I was angry at God and didn't want to hear from him. I was pretty sure his words wouldn't bring comfort to me because I was so angry.

Many of my friends recommended that I turn to God in my anger. They said he'd heal the hurt and wounds of my heart. But I'd built a wall, and it felt like nothing God could say could penetrate that wall or heal the wounds of my heart.

Have you ever been there? Where you've created a wall that stands right in front of God and your wellness?

The other thing that was interesting about this season was that in my heart of hearts, I knew God was present the entire time. I knew he was close. I knew that God in his nature wouldn't leave me, but I also knew I couldn't allow myself to hear from him in those moments.

Perhaps knowing that he wasn't going anywhere and that he promised to be "close to the brokenhearted" (Psalm 34:18) gave me the freedom, the space, and the time I needed to gain some critical distance from him, express my anger, and eventually shift to a new place in my relationship with him. His presence speaks of his confidence to bring about healing. His presence also poses the question Jesus asked the disabled man in John 5:6: "Do you want to get well?"

Jesus Invites Us to Be Healed

I just love the way Jesus woos us into a deeper relationship with him. Every interaction with him is an opportunity to know him and feel known and accepted by him. I also love how Jesus welcomes us to participate in matters that involve our own wellbeing. He doesn't force us to engage. He doesn't manipulate us into engaging. He invites us to join him. And then he leaves room for us to accept or decline interacting with him. I also love that Jesus doesn't simply offer us emotional healing; he offers us *total* healing. That includes physical and spiritual healing. Sometimes both happen this side of heaven; other times we wait in faith for Christ to return, knowing the rest of our healing will happen then.

In John 5, we meet Jesus in Jerusalem in an area one wouldn't think the promised King would be. If he was the holy Son of God, the Messiah, the creator of the universe, why was he not with dignitaries, executives, and kings, drinking expensive wine and eating lavish meals? Instead, Jesus sought out those whom society wouldn't give a second look: the sick, the helpless, the outcast, and the needy.

Read John 5:1-9 and picture yourself in the story:

Some time later [after healing an official's son while in Cana], Jesus went up to Jerusalem for one of the Jewish festivals. Now there is in Jerusalem near the Sheep Gate a pool, which in Aramaic is called Bethesda and which is surrounded by five covered colonnades. Here a great number of disabled people used to lie—the blind, the lame, the paralyzed. One who was there had been an invalid for thirty-eight years. When Jesus saw him lying there and learned that he had been in this condition for a long time, he asked him, "Do you want to get well?"

"Sir," the invalid replied, "I have no one to help me into the pool when the water is stirred. While I am trying to get in, someone else goes down ahead of me."

Then Jesus said to him, "Get up! Pick up your mat and walk." At once the man was cured; he picked up his mat and walked.

Reading this text compels me to ask several questions: What was this man's story? What had happened to him? Where were his family and friends? What resources did the community have to care for someone like him? Who were his advocates? Did anyone speak on his behalf? What would happen to him if no one stepped in to help?

When you read the question Jesus asked the disabled man—"Do you want to get well?"—position yourself in the story as the sick, the blind, the lame, the paralyzed, the traumatized. Do you feel their pain? Do you feel the weight of their challenges?

From the work I've done all around the world, it's clear that no one wants to be traumatized. No one asks for it, and they don't bring it on themselves. Sometimes their challenges began with family or relationship issues, and often our societies create structural categories that prevent the sick, blind, lame, paralyzed, and traumatized from rising above the bottom rung of the socioeconomic ladder. Do you feel the weight of their multilayered challenges?

Let's look at the disabled man's answer to Jesus' question before analyzing the question itself: "Sir, I have no one to help me into the pool when the water is stirred. While I am trying to get in, someone else goes down ahead of me" (verse 7). Many of us overlook this man's response and accuse him of making excuses for not being able to move fast enough to receive the healing that was available to him.

But I believe him. I don't know what kind of disability the man had, but let's assume it prevented him from moving at the pace of others. Let's assume that maybe others had intel he didn't have that would have helped him get to the front of the line fast enough. Let's assume that others had friends and family to help them get to the pool at just the right time, and he didn't. This man seemed to be the victim of many circumstances. If Jesus had not shown up at the right time, this man might have stayed in the same position for another thirty-eight years, or until his death.

The question *Do you want to get well?* is not intended to shame or blame victims or insinuate that the poor, homeless, and traumatized are in the situation they're in because of their own bad choices or decisions. Jesus' question meant something like *Do you believe that I AM the one who can bring healing to you and your situation right now?*

Throughout the book of John, that's the central question being asked and answered. In John 20:31, John states the point of his Gospel: "These [things] are written that you may believe that Jesus is the Messiah, the Son of God, and that by believing you may have life in his name." Jesus' posture toward the suffering and traumatized is patience, love, and compassion. He wants us to experience abundant life in his name, and he will not use shame or blame when he asks if we want to receive healing. He not only sympathizes with us but also empathizes, because he, too, experienced pain, suffering, and trauma on earth. He understands the knee of the system on his people's necks that renders them lifeless. Jesus gets close and stays close, as he has promised. He is patient until he finds the right opportunity to intervene and set us free.

Essential Steps for Saying Yes to Healing

I've heard a misconception in some Christian communities that those who are sick often remain that way because they are content in their circumstances or don't want help. I believe this is untrue and a harmful stance to take. I'd like to address this misconception and offer some guidance for helping those in need, especially to people in leadership positions or positions of power who can facilitate change.

Removing the Barriers

Two things must happen for the sick, blind, lame, paralyzed, and traumatized to be able to receive the healing they most desperately need. First, we need to understand the barriers that are keeping those in need from seeking help. And second, we need to work to remove those barriers.

Many people need help accessing the resources available to them. We can't assume that everyone has the same opportunities available to them. And we can't assume everyone has easy access to those opportunities. We must advocate for the removal of barriers so those in need can have access to the resources they need. Jesus stepped in and said to the disabled man, "I've removed the barriers for you. Now do you want to be healed? Do you want to be well?"

Even in the therapeutic space, there are barriers that make it difficult for those who need therapy to receive support. Finances are often one of the biggest deterrents to receiving support. Then there's navigating insurance companies. Even if you overcome these barriers, finding a therapist who will be a good match for your specific needs, personality, faith, race, and ethnicity is often an enormous undertaking. So how do we, like Jesus, remove the barriers so those in need have access to shalom, which is peace, wellness, wholeness, and prosperity?

Yes, many of us have built walls that prevent us from experiencing new life, but often these walls are there because of the suffering we've been through. Jesus understands. Some of us need a little more help.

Time and Space

Once the barriers are removed, some of us need time to develop and cultivate trust and figure out the kind of lives we desire on this earth. Some of us don't know how to even begin breaking down the walls so we can start healing. We each get to decide how much time we need before accepting the offer to be well. But rest assured, the invitation to heal is always around every corner we turn.

There have been seasons in my life when my walls prevented me from experiencing shalom. Henri Nouwen says that shalom is "well-being of mind, heart, and body, individually and communally."[1] Perhaps my heart was in such great lament and grief that I couldn't allow God to speak into the hurt. Perhaps I just needed space to sit in the pain. Perhaps I just needed time to accept what I couldn't understand. Either way, God was nearby, patiently waiting to offer me shalom. Perhaps we can use that same approach with those in need.

Most gracious God, we come to you by the power of the Holy Spirit, through Jesus' sacrifice on the cross and his resurrection, which give us the victory and freedom to pursue healing. God, we thank you for your love. We thank you for understanding our needs. We thank you for being patient with us. We thank you for not forcing us to enter places when we're not yet ready. We thank you for offering us healing. We thank you for being near. Father, we must admit that we don't know what the process of healing will look like. We pray that you will gently take us by the hand and do mighty work in our lives. We pray that you will bind the hands of the enemy, who wants to keep us in the cycle of hurt, pain, brokenness, and destruction. We pray that you will send a host of angels to watch over us and help us through this process. We desire a trusting relationship with you. And we desire shalom. Thank you for never leaving us or forsaking us. In Jesus' name we pray, amen!

QUESTIONS TO EXPLORE

1. Do you see yourself and your pain in the narrative about the disabled man in John 5? What resonates most with you?

2. What are the barriers in your life that prevent you from taking steps forward in your wellness journey? What do you need in order to begin breaking down the walls you've built?

3. Where is Jesus as you're dealing with this pain in your life?

4. What is he saying? Is there a question he's asking you? If so, what's the question, and what's your response?

5. Do you believe Jesus can make you well? Why, or why not?

FROM HEAD TO BODY

As Jesus shows you compassion, it's important to show yourself compassion, understanding, and love. A hug is a beautiful expression of comfort and compassion. It is also an intimate display of love. For the next exercise, give yourself a compassionate hug.

Begin by placing your right hand across your chest, near your heart, and gently pat your chest the way you would pat a child's back to assure them that everything will be okay. Give yourself a few more gentle taps. Then cross your left arm over your right arm, and place your left hand on your right shoulder. Hold this posture for as long as you need to feel safe, comforted, and loved.

PART TWO

FACING YOUR TRAUMA STORY

5

GRIEF

"Don't call me Naomi," she told [the women of Bethlehem].
"Call me Mara, because the Almighty has made my life very
bitter. I went away full, but the LORD has brought me back
empty. Why call me Naomi? The LORD has afflicted me;
the Almighty has brought misfortune upon me."

RUTH 1:20-21

My family experienced a traumatic and complex period of grief during Advent in 2019. Advent is a season before Christmas in which the universal church contemplates the gift of the Incarnation, when the Son of God "became flesh and made his dwelling among us" (John 1:14). So I was in a place of expectation and hope, desperate to see God and be reminded that there is a point and meaning to life on earth. However, just a few weeks before Advent season began, one of my youngest cousins died unexpectedly. He was my little brother's best friend, and we had grown up together. I admired him like a sibling. He and my brother were the only sons in their families, so they kept in regular contact.

I was extremely saddened after hearing of his unexpected passing. I supported the family from a distance and later flew home to New Jersey to be with my family and help officiate the funeral. My brother gave the eulogy and did a wonderful job of holding space for the family to grieve. Reflecting on the coming of Christ during Advent helped me hold on to the hope and assurance of being reunited with my cousin again one day. That hope helped me make peace with the loss of a loved one.

About a month passed, and early one morning, at about five o'clock, I heard groans coming from our living room. At first I thought I was dreaming, but then I quickly jumped out of bed to see who it was. When I reached the living room, I found my husband groaning in anguish. He was on the phone with our brother-in-law, who had just given him the news that my husband's twenty-year-old nephew had tragically died. I instantly lost my breath. Our families are close, and our children are around the same ages. With several others, they made up a group of nine cousins on my husband's side of the family. They even had their own cousins' chat group so they could speak freely away from the gaze of the granmouns ("older people").

The news threw each of us into a state of shock. We were unable to accept what was happening. We each began playing out the future in our heads, wondering how we would live in this world without our dear nephew. We all felt such deep sorrow for my nephew's parents, for his older sister, for our children, for their aunts and uncles, and for the extended family. The shock of his passing ran through our entire family like the outcry of the Egyptian families in the book of Exodus after losing their firstborn sons. Children in their prime should not die; they should live out their days and grow old. So we changed our plans for the holidays and once again joined the family, this time in Georgia, to lay our sweet nephew to rest in peace.

Hours before our nephew's wake, one of my older sisters arrived from out of town to pay her respects and attend the wake and funeral. My husband picked her up from the airport, and we met at the hotel to get dressed for the wake. My husband, my three sons, my cousin, my sister, and I all stepped into the elevator. I will never forget that ride as long as I live. My sister was on the phone with someone, and seconds after the elevator took off, the expression on her face changed completely. She looked as if she'd seen a ghost.

"Uh-oh," I joked. "Something serious has happened."

She was silent and emotionless.

Once we got off the elevator, I asked her what was wrong. She remained silent. After I prodded her, she finally said, "Sonny is dead."

Our little brother's name is Sonny, but my brain wasn't ready to accept the devastating news, so I asked, "Which Sonny?"

We knew only one Sonny, so I already knew the answer to my question.

"Our little brother," my sister replied, sobbing.

This was the first time as an adult that I consciously felt myself distancing from the emotional trauma so I could survive the next two weeks.

We had so much hope for the holidays. We had made plans and bought airline tickets. We were going to gather all our families in New Jersey for a week to celebrate Christmas together as we always did. We had cashed in our frequent flyer airline miles and planned a fabulous trip to Mexico after Christmas since we hadn't been on a family vacation in a while. But instead of celebrating Christmas or vacationing in Mexico, we planned and attended funerals. After my nephew's funeral in Georgia, we flew to New Jersey for my brother's funeral.

I once heard a preacher give a message on the book of Ruth. The topic of the message was the profound grief Naomi experienced following the death of her husband and sons in the land of Moab. When Naomi returned home to Bethlehem, she said to the women who greeted her, "Don't call me Naomi. . . . Call me

Mara, because the Almighty has made my life very bitter. I went away full, but the LORD has brought me back empty. Why call me Naomi? The LORD has afflicted me; the Almighty has brought misfortune upon me" (Ruth 1:20-21).

The preacher chastised Naomi for her attitude toward God during her season of grief. I instantly thought, *This preacher missed the point. He doesn't understand the nature of grief and God's posture toward the griever at all.*

When our family returned to Dallas after the funerals of our loved ones, Naomi's words were my only source of comfort. She gave me the language that helped normalize how I was feeling: "Call me bitter. . . . I went away full, but the LORD has brought me back empty." I felt empty. I had nothing to give. I felt cheated. I felt that God was cruel. I was traumatized. I was numb on most days and angry on other days. I felt as if I was floating through life, a shell of a person. Nothing felt comforting. Not music. Not TV. Not art. Creativity was snuffed out. I couldn't sleep in peace. And getting out of bed felt painful. I felt all alone. I felt empty. Hollow. I was deeply grieved.

I believe the multiple losses Naomi suffered were traumatic, and the grief she experienced was complex and profound, eliciting her bitter response. Losing close family and friends can be traumatic and complex, especially if multiple tragic and unexpected losses occur at the same time, or if there was any unresolved conflict with the deceased. I can make the case that Naomi's trauma included all these factors. No wonder she was bitter. I also believe she was a theologian with expertise on grief and lament, because thinking about God's intersection with human sorrow and suffering is theological work, and experiencing great suffering grants a person expertise on the subject.

Grief is an appropriate expression when we experience a loss of any kind, including of people, places, things, or expectations. You might experience the loss of a loved one, a marriage that ended in divorce, children who were never born, a marriage that never occurred, children who didn't live up to your expectations, the loss of physical health, the loss of savings, or a perfect career that ended prematurely. Grief is the deep sadness we feel when these things and people are no more.

Elisabeth Kübler-Ross is best known for her grief research. In her book *On Death and Dying*,[1] she discusses the five stages of grief that most people go through: denial, anger, bargaining (often with God), depression, and eventually acceptance. These stages help us understand the grieving process and the characteristics of each stage. However, most of us don't move through grief from one stage to the next in a linear way. For example, we might move back and forth through the stages, revisit a stage, or even skip a stage. Each person processes grief differently, so we shouldn't impose rigid expectations on those who are grieving. It's more helpful if we try to understand what they're going through and what they need. What's important in the grieving process is to keep moving through the journey, however long it takes.

Characteristics of the Grief Journey

In addition to these five stages, I experienced some other characteristics of grief during my season of loss. My own grief journey included shock and denial, anger, existential questioning and clarity, guilt and regret, wrestling with God, depression and sadness, stagnation, and acceptance and hope.

Shock and Denial

No other event can take your breath away quite like the unexpected death of a loved one. The event is so jarring that there's nowhere to fit it in your brain. Since my memory bank had no frame of reference for the unexpected deaths I experienced, I had no compartment for them. So the news of these deaths just floated around in my mind. I would often move in and out of shock, disbelief, and denial. A part of me simply couldn't believe this had happened. Sometimes denial is the only way we can cope with overwhelming loss and grief. Occasionally I would find myself moving to a place of accepting the loss only to end up back in shock and denial.

Anger

My anger following these losses was so raw that it scared me. I was afraid I'd never find my way out of it. I even distanced myself from people for fear that my anger would spill over onto them. But my anger was mostly directed toward God, because I felt he was cruel. In one of my journal entries during that season, I wrote, "I'm still very much angry at God. . . . I feel like I can't approach God to ask for anything. I can't ask for you not to take any more of my loved ones, because what's the point? You don't seem to care for what I want; you just seem to care about unleashing pain after pain on my life."

At the beginning of my grief journey, I was afraid to talk honestly with God about my feelings toward him. I was afraid I'd gone too far and wondered, *What if God gets angry back at me?* But none of those things happened. God was present. He wasn't so fragile that he couldn't take my anger. He wasn't spiteful. He gave me space to share, and he never left me.

Existential Questioning and Clarity

There's something about the grieving process that throws you into an existential crisis. You begin asking all kinds of questions about life and death. After the deaths of my loved ones, I suddenly found myself asking questions about the process of dying. What exactly happens when someone dies? What is this thing called life all about? What have I been doing with my life all this time? What is my purpose here on earth? With every question came greater clarity. I decided I didn't want to waste my time pursuing things that didn't matter in the bigger scheme of life. I wanted to live the rest of my days with more purpose. My priorities became more focused. I had a sense of urgency about living life more purposefully, robustly, and passionately.

Guilt and Regret

More often than not, those who are grieving a major loss feel as if they failed the deceased in some way. We might question whether we should have tried harder to preserve the lives of our loved ones or handled things differently. Guilt and regret often complicate the grieving process, especially if there were unresolved issues in the relationship or insufficient time to make peace and say goodbye. Cognitively, we know that if we could have done something to prevent our loved one's death, we would have. But when we're suffering, we may think we had more power over the situation than we actually did.

Wrestling with God

Apart from wrestling with the anger I felt in my grief, I found myself wrestling with the nature of God. Is God a good God? Or is he a cruel God who orchestrates suffering and death for his own pleasure? Both can't be true. I wrestled and wrestled with this. The process felt like a breakup with no other lover to turn to. After months of wrestling, I came to the realization that there was only one person in the equation with limited information: *me.* I could attest to the realness of God in my own life. And I knew that God is good because I had experienced his goodness personally and had seen it around the world. I also realized that I didn't know all there is to know. My understanding is limited, so I couldn't claim without a shadow of a doubt that God is cruel and finds pleasure in suffering and death. Though I still have questions about how and why God allowed what happened with my brother and nephew, all my wrestling eventually led to a resolve that there is a God who is good, who loves me, and who desires for me to flourish.

Depression and Sadness

After all the rage and wrestling with God in a desperate effort to figure things out, I entered a season of depression. Depression was a welcome break from the intensity of my emotions. During this season, I often felt numb and found I had less energy to fight through the other emotions I was experiencing.

Sadness and depression go hand in hand, but sadness is an emotion that many of us have a hard time identifying or naming. Sadness is one of the characteristics of depression. At the center of sadness, you will find despair, sorrow, grief, and loss. Underneath all the other emotions I was experiencing, I felt a deep sadness. Our anger can be so loud that we may not hear the sadness. We may feel sadness as we realize that our loved ones will no longer be a part of our lives. Or as we face a new reality—a new normal without our loved ones.

Stagnation

Stagnation is the point of feeling stuck and unable to make progress on your journey ahead. It may feel like procrastination or even laziness. But it's neither one of those things. It's a very real part of the grief journey. During this phase of my grief, I was stuck. I didn't know how to pick up the pieces and move forward with my life. I became afraid that I wouldn't find my way out. My anxiety increased as I struggled to break free from the stagnation of grief and find new meaning in life. I had to keep reminding myself to breathe and stop fighting the grief, to just let it be. I had to wait for God to show me how to continue my grief journey while I learned to move forward in life. In the waiting, I learned that grieving your loved one never ends, but God's loving presence empowered me to live out my calling with an even greater sense of urgency.

Acceptance and Hope

In the beginning, the grief journey is like a roller coaster thrusting you about with no end in sight. Acceptance seems to fall at the very end: Your pain subsides, and you are able to better embrace your reality. However, what I've realized is that acceptance and hope are often sprinkled throughout the journey. Acceptance and hope can come in small doses, or we can experience a season where we feel hopeful about life again, only to feel shock and sadness all over again. And that's okay and very normal. I have found that the best way to navigate the grief journey is by allowing hope and acceptance to come naturally, with hands wide open, ready to receive hope wherever and whenever it shows up.

Tips for the Grieving Process

Beloved sisters, don't fight the grief journey; allow theologians like Naomi to show you the way forward. Let the tears come as they may. Let the sadness rest on you like a blanket on a cold day. Let angry words flow toward God, because he is safe and welcomes your full self, messy and all. In the end, you will find comfort in the loving arms of God—but the process will be tough, and you can't forget to take care of your needs. Here are some tips to guide you as you grieve:

- Take care of yourself: Drink water, breathe, and walk. Honor yourself by being present and paying attention to your needs.

- Don't grieve alone. This is a season when having a healthy community around you is of utmost importance. Ask for help and let others help you. Find safe people to communicate your needs to.

• When you're ready, set up an appointment with a grief counselor or a grief support group like GriefShare. I also recognize that in many cultures and communities, grief support is more communal and not as formal as a GriefShare group. My advice is to use the community resources that are available to you.

• If you're depressed or anxious or haven't been able to sleep for an extended period of time, call your doctor for help. When you're grieving, there is always a possibility you will get stuck, depressed, and anxious at some point on this journey. So be aware and get help when or if you do.

• There's nothing wrong with resuming your normal activities, like going back to work right away. The routine might be just what you need to help you keep it somewhat together. Everything doesn't need to fall apart when you're grieving.

I've learned that grieving takes time. We're constantly navigating loss and grief throughout our lives, whether the losses are big or small. While grief doesn't go away, our relationship with it can become less strained. A dear sister once told me, "Grief is an animal we live with. Wild at first, and then gradually it gets domesticated, but it never becomes a beloved pet." Take your time learning to live with it.

Jesus, in your humanity, you became well acquainted with grief and loss, so you understand our grief. Be with your daughters on this grief journey. Remind them that they are safe with you and that nothing can separate them from the love you have for them. Let them know that you are present. Nestle them in your loving arms. Comfort them in a way that gives them the strength to take steps forward. We pray this in your powerful name, amen.

QUESTIONS TO EXPLORE

1. Whom or what are you grieving? Share more about your grief.

2. Is there a biblical figure who speaks of grief in a way that resonates with you? If so, what do you relate to most about their story or message?

3. Do you identify with any of the grief characteristics we talked about? Which ones? What others would you add?

4. What do you need as you grieve? If you feel stuck in your grief, unable to make any progress, take some time to identify what you need in this season to keep moving forward. Make a list of people you know who could help you meet those needs.

5. What has helped you take steps forward in your grief? What does moving forward look like to you? How would you categorize it?

6. How are you taking care of yourself as you grieve?

FROM HEAD TO BODY

Honor your grief journey. All around the world, there are rituals, practices, and activities that help make the intangible tangible and give the griever permission to grieve. People express their grief differently in each culture. In some cultures, they wear certain colors or invite wailers to join them in lament. In other cultures, the community is invited to join in the grieving, and the mourners bring food and gifts. In many cultures, the bereaved visit the graves of their loved ones.

In some cultures, Christians frown upon these rituals and practices out of fear. In Haiti, for example, many Christians frown upon visiting cemeteries or the gravesites of the deceased because they fear a connection to voodoo practices and ancestor worship. While some practices may involve voodoo or ancestor worship, many are, in fact, biblical and God honoring. In the Bible, God commanded the people to gather stones as memorials of his faithfulness (Joshua 4). In fact, throughout the Bible, we are encouraged over and over to remember what God has done in our lives.

Rituals aid us in remembering someone we have lost or something profound that has happened so that we won't forget and leave the person or experience behind. It's a way of taking that person or experience with us through the rest of our journey so that even in their passing, they might continue to minister to us.

It doesn't mean you're any less of a Christian if you are part of a culture that provides a way for you to grieve. It does not mean you're inviting Satan into your grief journey. I'm mindful that Jesus, too, was from a culture that created space for grieving and celebration in the form of rituals, practices, and activities.

Here are some tangible ways you can honor your grief journey by laying down a stone of remembrance:

- Create a memorial garden.
- Light a candle in memory of the person or experience.
- Visit the grave of your loved one.
- Release balloons as a memorial.
- Wear something special to honor your loved one, like their favorite sneakers.
- Make a T-shirt.
- Go on a memorial walk.
- Run a memorial race.

If you're grieving a loss outside of death, such as the loss of a friendship, a marriage, or a job, you will still go through a grieving process. And you will need to honor your grief journey, though it might look different from grieving the death of a loved one.

Tangible practices like these can help you communicate an intangible ending and step into a new beginning:

- Get rid of items that connect you with the past. This process can be cleansing and rejuvenating.
- Clean and reorganize your space.
- Move to a new place to live, work, and worship. Starting over somewhere else can help you move forward.
- Start a new project or hobby to feel a sense of empowerment.
- Tap into your creativity by giving yourself the freedom to explore.

6

SHAME

Instead of your shame there shall be a double portion;
  instead of dishonor they shall rejoice in their lot;
therefore in their land they shall possess a double portion;
  they shall have everlasting joy.

ISAIAH 61:7, ESV

During my season of grief over my unexpected pregnancy out of wedlock, the dominant emotion I felt was shame. Not only did I feel exposed and horrible, but everywhere I turned, people in my community were communicating the same message: "You are not enough because you didn't live according to our rules." They couldn't seem to think of any other way to engage with me other than shame. And shame did exactly what it aimed to do: It left me feeling alone, broken, and like less of a human being. I felt like I didn't deserve to breathe the same air as those who had it all together and lived their lives according to the standards of the community. So I reasoned that I deserved mistreatment and punishment and should not be shown mercy or love.

More than anything, shame communicates that we are not enough.

We're not smart enough. We're not pretty enough. We're not spiritual enough. We're not holy enough. We're not enough as singles. We're not enough as spouses. We're not enough as parents. We're not enough as providers. We're not enough as daughters, sisters, or friends. We're not enough as human beings.

We are never enough.

We are not worthy to exist and take up space on this earth.

So we hide, we shrink, we hold back, and we become less while seeking every opportunity to prove that we are enough.

The Face of Shame

Brené Brown says,

> I define shame as the intensely painful feeling or experience of believing that we are flawed and therefore unworthy of love and belonging—something we've experienced, done, or failed to do makes us unworthy of connection.
>
> I don't believe shame is helpful or productive. In fact, I think shame is much more likely to be the source of destructive, hurtful behavior than the solution or cure. I think the fear of disconnection can make us dangerous.[1]

Shame is not helpful. If anything, the fear of shame has resulted in many unhelpful decisions in my life. Social pressures like those I experienced in my church and community often create an atmosphere in which shame thrives. Shame and the fear it evokes squelch the Spirit of God in each of us. Shame causes us to shrink and lose our unique voices in our search for approval that we'll never receive. Shame suppresses creativity. It often suffocates freedom and oppresses our spirits.

The Antidote to Shame

Throughout my years as a counselor and pastor ministering to women around the world, I've heard many stories of women like me who have felt the weight of shame. I want to elevate their voices to help us see what shame looks like and what it does to us. Brown says that the antidote to shame is to bring it out of the shadows, speak of it openly, and address it with empathy. "Shame cannot survive being spoken . . . and being met with empathy," she points out.[2]

Over the years I've seen how this principle is applied in real life. When shame is brought into the light and the hearer responds with empathy, it softens the heart. It's as if you're receiving a tender emotional hug. Shame demands punishment and destroys our sense of identity and belonging. When people respond empathetically, it is a shock to our system, prompting a reactionary set of questions: "Why are you not participating with others and shaming me the way I've always felt and heard I deserved? Why are you responding with kindness?" Many times, the shamed break down in tears because a stronghold has been torn down. And the lie that we aren't worthy of grace and love vanishes the moment the shameful secret is revealed. The simple exposure of that shame to the light brings a measure of healing on its own.

We experience healing when our stories of shame are met with empathy.

- To the women who are unmarried and are told they're not enough and will never be enough until they get married and have children: Your pain is seen and heard. If or when you decide to marry and have children, I pray it will be your own decision and not a result of societal pressures. You are loved as you are.

- To the women who have been told they are bad mothers and didn't do enough to discipline children who have made life decisions that have ended painfully: God sees your efforts and hears your cries for your shame to be lifted. You did the best you could with what you knew at the time. Your children's choices are not your own. Keep loving your children and speaking life into them. You are enough and necessary.

- To the abused woman or girl who has been blamed for her abuse and told that she shouldn't have dressed that way, shouldn't have gone to that neighborhood, should have fought back, and maybe even liked it: It was not your fault. You are not to blame. You did not cause what happened to you. You are allowed to live, breathe, and walk freely without the threat of abuse. God sees you, hears you, and accepts you. He is restoring you and breathing new life into you.

- To the women whose husbands have been unfaithful and are told that if they had cooked for their husbands, kept a clean house, created a peaceful environment, and pleasured them enough sexually, they wouldn't have strayed: God sees you and knows that trauma and brokenness have layers and sometimes those layers spill over into relationships, creating complications in your marriage. You are worthy of a mutually loving relationship based on faithfulness and respect. You are worth fighting for. God is walking with you as you heal.

- To the women who have been physically abused and are told it is their fault because they didn't leave the relationship when it became violent: My heart aches for you. I'm sorry we live in a world that perpetuates violence against women and makes it difficult to seek support. You are not alone in this journey of healing. You are worth being in a relationship free of violence. You have permission to seek help and support, whether it's your first or fifth time seeking help. God sees you and is with you as you fight for a flourishing future.

- To the women in prison who have been told they are too broken to ever become someone in life: As you read this book, I invite you to step into your own healing journey. You are not too broken for mercy and love. The invitations are all around you. You have what you need to take one step and the next. God sees you, walks with you, and gives you strength as you keep moving forward.

- To the women in Haiti and other developing countries who have been told to stop begging and being so needy when you were only doing the best you could to survive and preserve the lives of your children: God sees your efforts and commends you. You are a fighter, stopping at nothing to ensure that the next generation gets a chance at life. Look up and see the presence of God with you and throughout your story. Thank you for preserving my life.

- To the Black women from the African diaspora who are told they're not Black enough, they don't belong, and they're not true natives of their homelands: I see you. I hear you. You belong. You are a child of the world, a child of God. Your story of coming into your Black woman self matters. You are loved with all your layers.

- To Black women, Indigenous women, and other women of color who are told they must conform to a specific standard of beauty: You were not created to fit into a specific mold. God sees you. You were created uniquely and beautifully on purpose. God did not make a mistake creating you with different features. You will never fully align with distorted standards, so rely on the One who created you and called you good, worthy, and loved. Proudly wear your crown and step into your healing journey.

Can you think of your own shame scenarios? You probably can, since the shame narrative is strong and loud. It's important to be aware of its voice and put it to rest every day with empathy and love for yourself. In my journey of healing, I have found that love trumps shame.

What Do You Want?

While most people in my immigrant community didn't know how to embrace me without shaming me, there were a few outliers. One of them was my older sister Angie. When she saw the weight of shame I was carrying, she asked a simple question: "What do you want?"

That was such a remarkable and symbolic question. Black women are rarely asked what they'd like to do, even in matters that directly impact us. Decisions are often made for us. We have to fight to be heard, believed, and respected. Maybe that's why Hagar—and the Samaritan woman at the well in John 4—seemed surprised that God even cared about what she wanted. Maybe for the first time in their lives, someone cared enough to ask them a question, listen for the answer, and then provide for their needs.

My sister not only asked what I wanted, but she also listened to my response and made sure my wishes were honored. That question was an essential part of my healing process; it communicated, "I see you. I respect you. I honor you." Feeling known, seen, and respected gave me the strength I needed to go on. I saw a glimpse of hope. I suspect this is why Hagar exclaimed, "You are El Roi, the God who sees me" (Genesis 16:13, PAR). The right question is catalytic in the healing journey. It was for me, for Hagar, and for the woman at the well.

Another pair of outliers in my shame narrative was a couple who had been childhood friends of mine. They didn't follow the trajectory of the shaming culture. They came to visit and sit with me. They brought a card sharing words of encouragement. I felt their love and acceptance.

And then there was a good college friend. I was so sick from the pregnancy that it was hard to attend classes and take care of myself. She came to my dorm room and straightened things up for me. She swept my floors and cleaned my room. She took care of me, greased my scalp, and fixed my hair. She took time to love me. I've always joked with her that if we ever made it on *The Oprah Winfrey Show*, this would be the story we'd share.

Empathy and love heal. The love I experienced more than twenty years ago in the midst of my shame continues to transform me as I pastor and counsel others, and in every relationship I encounter. It reminds me to give the same empathy and love to others in their time of need.

May you find communities and people who communicate that you are enough. May you daily connect through the Holy Spirit with the God who made you enough.

Father, when Adam and Eve recognized their shame and nakedness in the garden, you provided a covering for them. Would you please do the same for us? We know that your Son, Jesus Christ, provided the covering for our shame through his life, death, and resurrection. Would you help us live in the truth of his sacrifice, which washes away our shame? Would you draw others to come alongside us to offer empathy rather than judgment and remind us of your love and acceptance? Would you remind us daily of the truth of who we are when shame shows up to drag us down? Father, free us from shame so we can live out our purpose, for your name's sake. Amen.

QUESTIONS TO EXPLORE

1. What is your shame narrative?

2. How do you feel when it starts playing in your mind?

3. How do you put it to rest?

4. What truths do you practice that help you combat your shame narrative?

5. Has anyone modeled empathy and love in your time of need? How did it impact you?

FROM HEAD TO BODY

Positive affirmations are one of the keys to healing. Unfortunately, they have been receiving a bad rep in Christian circles, partly because many believe they're too surfacy and that they have no basis in Scripture. What if I told you that positive affirmations are modeled after our Creator God? Genesis 1 tells us that after God had created the earth, he looked around, admiring what he had created, and declared it "very good" (verse 31).

So speaking positively about ourselves is a method from God's own book. Positive affirmations acknowledge God's goodness in our lives. Affirming ourselves is the discipline of accepting what God says about us instead of believing the lies of the shame narrative.

This week, focus on your shame narrative whenever it shows up, and write down what it says. And each time it shows up, counter it with positive affirmations about yourself, using "I am" statements. If you like, include verses from the Bible in your affirmations. Make sure to write these affirmations in your journal so you can reference them in the future.

Here is an example:

Shame narrative: You're not good enough, you will never be good enough, and you can't do anything right.

Affirmation: God created me with purpose, and I am enough. I'm a work in progress. I will do all that God has called me to, one day at a time.

Notice how you're responding emotionally to these affirmations and track your progress daily.

DOMESTIC VIOLENCE

[Abram] slept with Hagar, and she conceived.
When she knew she was pregnant, she began to despise her
mistress. Then Sarai said to Abram, "You are responsible
for the wrong I am suffering. I put my slave in your arms,
and now that she knows she is pregnant, she despises
me. May the LORD judge between you and me."
"Your slave is in your hands," Abram said. "Do
with her whatever you think best." Then Sarai
mistreated Hagar; so she fled from her.

GENESIS 16:4-6

During one of my trauma-healing trips to Haiti, I stopped by a ministry partner called Heartline to speak to a group of expectant mothers. The focus of their ministry is to preserve the Haitian family by offering maternal care and helping expectant mothers deliver their babies safely.

Usually after I speak, women will line up wanting to connect with me about their unique situations. This time was no different. One woman came up and told me she was new to the ministry. Then she began telling me her story. When she became pregnant, her husband was upset and blamed her because he didn't want another child. He began beating her, hoping she'd lose the baby. One night the beating was so bad, she thought she'd lose not only the child but her life as well. She screamed loudly, knowing the neighbors would hear her and hoping they would intervene, but no one did. When she consulted with her pastor at church, he told her to avoid making her husband mad and to continue cooking, cleaning, and being kind to him. She tried all those things, but her husband continued the abuse. She told me the only thing that helped her was telling him that if she had the baby, he would not have to help support them financially. She later found Heartline, which she believed was an answer to her prayers.

Out of grad school, I interned at a domestic violence facility that offered shelter, education, counseling, and other resources for women and their families as they reeled from the trauma of domestic violence. There I learned that domestic violence usually begins as most other relationships do: with love. Most women would run if their relationships started with abuse and trauma—especially women with privilege who don't need the income of a partner to survive.

For many, there is a honeymoon phase when the relationship is running smoothly. Then over time, the dynamic of the relationship changes and escalates to emotional and physical violence. Sometimes the pressures of life under the patriarchal umbrella, unresolved trauma from the past, and mental-health challenges create the perfect atmosphere for violence against women. Adding to the problem are societal pressures dictating that women find their worth in a marital relationship. To escape the shame of a troubled relationship, women often present to the world the illusion of having a perfect family and suffer alone in silence.

Another aspect of domestic violence that makes it even more confusing, painful, and hard to heal from is the posture of the person inflicting the abuse. The one responsible for the domestic violence is often an intimate partner who once professed to love and care for the woman he later abuses. Claims of love are then used to manipulate the woman into submission and staying in the relationship. Many women are entangled in a repeating cycle of love, lies, violence, and empty promises because love is intertwined with the hope that their partners will change without any tangible interventions.

As a society, we often have many misconceptions regarding domestic violence. We assume that this issue affects only the uneducated, poor, marginalized, or otherwise vulnerable in society. Some even equate domestic violence with people of color. We tend to think that communities with wealth or power are immune. The reality is that domestic violence is a problem all women face across the globe, regardless of education, race, and socioeconomic status.

Getting to the Core

Researchers and mental-health professionals who work with victims of abuse have learned that power and control are at the core of every form of domestic violence. Power and control are also key considerations in systems of patriarchy, where men lead and rule.

Confronting domestic violence is more challenging when biblical texts are mishandled. In many religious circles, men are assigned absolute authority over the household, and women are expected to unquestioningly submit and follow their leadership. That patriarchal interpretation is often attributed directly to God.

Angela Parker calls this *irrational reverence*. In her book *If God Still Breathes, Why Can't I?*, she explains that "irrational reverence means folks begin to use the Bible not as a conversation starter but as a conversation ender." She continues: "Think of the phrase 'the Bible says' and how it is often considered the be-all and end-all in an argument. The biblical text becomes a bludgeoning tool used to exert supremacist authoritarianism; what the Bible says (or rather, how the wielder interprets what the Bible says) goes."[1] I have seen what can happen in households where there is a rigid theological understanding of men having the power and control and women having no agency. Not only can this lead to domestic violence taking place within the home, but it can also mean limited measures of accountability because "the Bible says."

In her book *Redeeming Power: Understanding Authority and Abuse in the Church*, Diane Langberg says this about power: "Exploiting our position in the home or the church to get our own way, serve our own ends, crush others, silence them, and frighten them is a wrong use of power. Using our influence or our reputation to get others to further our own ends is a wrong use of power. Withholding power in the face of sin, abuse, and tyranny is also a wrong use of power. It is sin against God—complicity with the evil he hates."[2]

At the center of domestic violence, you will find power and control that seek to dominate for the sake of dominance, leaving no room for women to have agency and ultimately flourish. We need a theology based on love, respect, and mutuality. A theology that creates the atmosphere for all God's children to thrive and flourish, women and men.

I often hear the question "Why do women stay in abusive relationships?" This question almost always lands judgmentally. It's as if the person is saying, "You must be stupid for staying in such a toxic relationship." It's also a shaming question and a major deterrent that makes it hard for women to seek help and support.

Women stay for a host of reasons. Financially, many women find it too difficult to start over and earn enough income to take care of themselves and in many cases their children as well. Emotionally, women often have a hard time leaving intimate partners when there's domestic violence. A woman in an abusive relationship may be too afraid to leave. Or maybe she met her partner during a vulnerable time in her life. Perhaps she and her partner grew up together. Or maybe this partner once helped her out in a meaningful way, and she feels indebted to him. Sometimes the emotional entanglement is so profound that women become frozen, unable to remove themselves from the very relationship that is inflicting harm on them.

In some cultures, it's allowed and acceptable for husbands to beat their wives and emotionally abuse them into submission. I want to challenge these culturally accepted norms and call the people of God to live above culture. Christ is our ultimate example. He is our ultimate guide, and he leads with grace and love, not striving for power and control. No household should follow cultural norms above Christ's example.

Naming the Signs

Women from all over the world know what love is, what it feels like, and how they should be treated. What often keeps them from expressing those needs is a society obsessed with debasing women while nurturing an atmosphere where violence can flourish. We live in a society obsessed with power and control, and the thought of losing these things often leads to violence. As humans, we are created to respond to love, respect, and compassion in all our relationships.

When I ask women about naming the signs that a relationship is unhealthy and possibly unsafe, this is what they say:

- "You are put down and embarrassed."
- "Your partner encourages you to stay away from friends and family."
- "You're subjected to verbal abuse, name-calling, put-downs, insults, invalidation, and gaslighting."
- "Your partner takes money from you, makes you ask for money, and hides money and other resources from you."

- "Your partner controls whom you see, where you go, and what you do."
- "Your partner looks at you in an intimidating manner."
- "Your partner intimidates you with weapons."
- "Your partner threatens to assault you."
- "Your partner pressures you to have sex when you don't want to or forces you to engage in sexual acts you're uncomfortable with."
- "Your partner uses your children against you or threatens to take them away or hurt them."
- "Your partner forces you to get pregnant or have an abortion."
- "Your partner physically abuses you by pushing, shoving, punching, or kicking you."

All over the world, there is great consensus among women about how they *don't* want to be treated. They know that violence in a relationship is unjust even when many don't have the power or resources to get out of those kinds of relationships.

Relationships should be based on mutual love and respect, not power and control. Whenever I teach and counsel on this subject, I usually spend some time asking women to name the values they desire in their relationships.

This is what many of them say they want:

- "Someone who treats me well and is kind."
- "Someone who looks out for me."
- "Someone who supports me and encourages me."
- "Someone who listens to me."
- "Someone who respects my desires and wishes."
- "Someone who isn't afraid of my emotions."
- "A person who allows me to dream and encourages me to be my true self and go after my dreams."

- "A true partnership where we make decisions together."
- "A person who knows the Lord and has a relationship with him."

A Holistic Approach to Freedom from Violence

For women to receive the help and support they need to live in freedom from violent relationships, we need a holistic approach to the problem. First, we need educational programs that create awareness. Churches, nonprofit organizations, and for-profit organizations must all be educated to break the cycle of silence and shame. They need to be trauma informed and offer resources and options for women experiencing domestic violence.

Second, women need options that will enable them to safely leave violent relationships when they are ready. I've learned that the most dangerous day in a woman's life is the day she decides to leave a violent relationship. Third, we need to advocate for laws that protect women and children from violence and prosecute offenders to keep women safe. Last, we must challenge religious communities to reconsider their use of certain biblical texts that are used to keep women in dangerous relationships. Their rigidity on preserving the family while overlooking violence within the family has proved to be dangerous for women and their children.

When Hagar's mistress, Sarai, mistreated her, Hagar ran away to preserve her life and the life of her unborn child. I don't know what happened to the woman I met in Haiti. Knowing the ministry of Heartline, I'm sure she received great care and support throughout her pregnancy. But like Hagar, she had to fight to preserve her life and the life of her unborn child. I pray that like Hagar and the woman I met in Haiti, we will be women who fight not only to ensure our own safety and the safety of our children but also to support other women in breaking the cycle of domestic violence. I pray for a world where women can live in freedom from violence.

God, we call on your name. Hear the prayers of our hearts. Protect and provide for our every need. For women who are stuck and unable to get out of dangerous situations, God, make a way. Be present and speak mightily on their behalf. Make a way, dear God. Show up through friends and unexpected sources to provide the help they need. We trust in your unfailing love and provision. Make a way, oh Lord. Amen.

‡

If you are currently going through some form of domestic violence and are unsafe, I'm sorry. I grieve with you and for you. You are not alone. I'm sure that at this point you have tried everything you can to create peace and a loving partnership to no avail. Changing your circumstances will be challenging, especially if you have children, and it will involve many steps. But it is not impossible.

The first step is to assess the resources and support your family and community can provide. I understand that not all resources will be safe, but it is important to identify safe people who can help you create a plan to leave this unsafe situation. If you're unable to leave for financial reasons, or any other reason, create a strategy that will help you and your children live free from violence. Part of that plan must include saving money and concealing it in a private location so that when the time is right, you can leave without fearing insufficient finances. Remember to turn to your community for support during this transition. As a child of God created in his image, you are worthy of love and respect and a relationship that is free from emotional and physical violence.

If you need additional support, I would encourage you to reach out to one of the following organizations:

National Domestic Violence Hotline: 1-800-799-7233
National Human Trafficking Hotline: 1-888-373-7888

QUESTIONS TO EXPLORE

My hope is that the following questions will help you take an honest look at your present reality, find the language to describe it, and discern your next steps in the healing journey.

1. How did you meet your partner?

2. What were your values and hopes for the relationship?

3. When did the nature of the relationship change?

4. When did you become aware that there was a problem in the relationship?

5. What were the red flags in the relationship?

6. What is your present reality?

7. What has made it hard for you to break free from this relationship?

8. If you have gotten out, how did you do it?

9. If you have not gotten out, what do you need to help you take that step?

FROM HEAD TO BODY

As we've seen in this chapter, power and control are at the center of domestic violence and other oppressive systems that debase women. So I want you to practice reclaiming your power by engaging in some kind of exercise or sports activity. These activities can strengthen not only your physical body but your mind as well. Challenge yourself by creating an exercise routine, setting a goal, and tracking your progress week by week. Start slow and gradually increase your time, number of repetitions, and intensity, depending on the exercise.[3]

Here are some examples to get you started:

- Walk for five to ten minutes at a park or in the community where you live.

- Jog lightly for five to ten minutes.

- Do some squats, starting with three or four sets of six to eight reps. (*Note:* A rep, or repetition, is a single squat that you perform within a cycle. A set is a series of reps. So for each set, you would perform six to eight squats.)

- Do some lunges on each side, starting with three or four sets of six to eight reps.

- Do three or four wall sits for twenty seconds each.

- Do fifteen or twenty sit-ups.

8

SEXUAL ABUSE

In his very nature he was God.
Jesus was equal with God. But Jesus didn't take
advantage of that fact.
Instead, he made himself nothing.
He did this by taking on the nature of a servant.
He was made just like human beings.
He appeared as a man.
He was humble and obeyed God completely.
He did this even though it led to his death.
Even worse, he died on a cross!

PHILIPPIANS 2:6-8, NIrV

Earlier in the book, I shared about a woman I met while ministering in jail. She had always dreamed of becoming an Olympic gold medalist as a child. However, the odious act of childhood sexual abuse destroyed her dream. That abuse and the traumatic impact it had on her life eventually led to her incarceration. Sexual trauma not only destroys dreams; it shatters lives and changes who we are.

I once heard a therapist use the analogy that sexual trauma is like dynamite exploding inside us. When that dynamite detonates, it shatters everything in sight, making it difficult to put all the pieces back together again.

Sexual abuse disrupts the lives of its victims. It creates confusion and distortions in our relationships with ourselves, God, and others, especially when it occurs at a young age.

Growing up, I never heard anyone talk about sexual abuse or share their own stories—not in my family or the community and certainly not in the church. It wasn't until my adult years that I started meeting women who shared openly about their sexual abuse.

There are a number of reasons why most of us never hear stories of sexual abuse. First of all, most victims of sexual abuse will not openly share their stories because of shame and the stigma associated with being a victim of abuse. It is estimated that 20 percent of women are sexually abused in their lifetime,[1] and approximately 70 percent of victims never report the abuse to anyone.[2]

Second, our societal structures discourage women from reporting sexual abuse. Even when incidents are reported, the victims' stories often aren't believed or given the attention they deserve. Looking back, my sense is that my community worked hard to keep claims of sexual abuse swept under a rug. Instead, people seemed to prefer the narrative that sexual abuse wasn't occurring in our communities, families, and even our churches. I think that most people would rather pretend that sexual abuse isn't happening, because this crime is so heinous and vile. We want to believe that the propensity for that kind of evil couldn't possibly reside in us or in members of our communities and churches. I also believe that censoring and suppressing stories of sexual trauma is a way of protecting the powerful and the systems that benefit them. It ensures that they won't have to submit to authority and be held accountable for their actions.

Fear often prevents us from hearing the real-life stories of women and girls who have been violated sexually. We are afraid of what could happen if we disrupt the system that protects those who engage in sexual violence. What would happen to the illusion of safety we have created if we exposed the evil of sexual abuse to the light?

Tamar's Story

I remember the first time I became acquainted with a victim of sexual abuse. That encounter wasn't in person; it was in the pages of the Bible. Tamar was a beautiful young woman from the family of David who became a victim of sexual violence. And the perpetrator was her brother. Her story is found in 2 Samuel 13:1-22.

The main people in this passage are Amnon and Absalom, who were both sons of David. It is interesting that the author introduced Tamar as Absalom's sister, not as King David's daughter. We can also instantly observe who had power and who didn't.

In her book *Texts of Terror*, Phyllis Trible writes, "Two males surround a female. As the story unfolds, they move between protecting and polluting, supporting and seducing, comforting and capturing her."[3] In Tamar's life, Absalom was the protector, supporter, and comforter, while Amnon was the polluter, seducer, and capturer. Caught between these two forces, Tamar didn't stand a chance. She had no agency over her body; they chose the disastrous outcome for her. Amnon sexually assaulted her. David, their father, did not hold Amnon accountable for raping her. Absalom waited two years before committing his vengeful murder, telling Tamar to "'be quiet. . . . Don't take this thing to heart.' And Tamar lived in her brother Absalom's house, a desolate woman" (2 Samuel 13:20). The power over her fate was never hers.

As I was reflecting on Tamar's story, I was reminded of the story of another young girl. Like Tamar, this young girl had no agency over her body or her life. She also had a protector and someone who violated her. Both protector and perpetrator were within the family. The perpetrator of her rape was her mother's live-in boyfriend. And similar to Tamar's story, someone in her family allegedly killed the perpetrator in an act of revenge. This was the story of Maya Angelou, which she writes about in her acclaimed book *I Know Why the Caged Bird Sings*. After her perpetrator was killed, young Maya became mute. The sheer magnitude of the trauma, shame, and humiliation she suffered caused her to retreat inward and stop speaking to anyone in the outside world except her brother, Bailey.

Both stories rightly represent the nature of sexual abuse. For starters, sexual abuse often occurs in the context of the family. This context creates easy access for abuse to take place. The family provides the atmosphere for coercion and manipulation. In the family, we often see unbalanced power dynamics that are hierarchical and patriarchal. These dynamics give absolute power, first, to the male figures and, second, to the eldest in the family. So when rape occurs in the family, the priority is usually to protect the one with the most power. The one with the most power is often believed over the one with the least power. Fear of disrupting the family system can lead to silence, creating even more trauma for victims. One thing is clear about sexual abuse: An atmosphere for abuse is fostered in familial relationships where those with the least power have no agency to enforce boundaries.

Victims typically reexperience the trauma of sexual abuse for years as the shattering of boundaries continues to impact them. Many carry the weight of shame as they constantly replay the traumatic events and wonder what they could have done differently to prevent the abuse from occurring in the first place. Many become hypervigilant, always on high alert as their internal alarm systems rationally scan for danger. And many experience distrust in their relationships with God, themselves, and others. This is why we must address the power dynamics underlying the kind of trauma that lingers long after the sexual abuse has taken place.

Imbalance and Abuse of Power

Sexual abuse is a crime that is correlated with an imbalance and abuse of power. According to RAINN (the Rape, Abuse, and Incest National Network), there are three key forms of criminal sexual abuse that involve assertions of power: sexual assault, rape, and force.[4]

Sexual assault is defined as "sexual contact or behavior that occurs without explicit consent of the victim." Examples of sexual assault are "attempted rape, fondling or unwanted sexual touching, forcing a victim to perform sexual acts, such as oral sex or penetrating the perpetrator's body, and penetration of the victim's body, also known as rape."

The second form of sexual assault is rape, but as RAINN points out, "Not all sexual assault is rape." According to the legal definition, rape specifically includes "sexual penetration without consent." The FBI defines *rape* as "penetration, no matter how slight, of the vagina or anus with any body part or object, or oral penetration by a sex organ of another person, without the consent of the victim."

Force is the third form of sexual assault. According to RAINN, force isn't always physical, and I agree. Here's how they describe it: "Force doesn't always refer to physical pressure. Perpetrators may use emotional coercion, psychological force, or manipulation to coerce a victim into non-consensual sex. Some perpetrators will use threats to force a victim to comply, such as threatening to hurt the victim or their family or other intimidation tactics."

In each of these descriptions is the underlying theme of power.

Power used for selfish gain. Power used to take advantage without consent. Power used to dominate emotionally and physically. Sexual abuse comes from the imbalance and abuse of power.

As I look at these definitions and revisit well-known biblical narratives, many more women besides just Tamar come to mind whose stories would fit under the categories of sexual abuse, assault, or trauma. Hagar's experience, for example, would most certainly fit under the category of sexual trauma. As a trafficked foreign slave, she had no agency over her body, no right to give or withhold consent.

In her book *Hagar, Sarah, and Their Children*, Phyllis Trible observes that "Hagar the Egyptian is single, poor, and slave but also young and fertile. Power belongs to Sarai; powerlessness marks Hagar."[5] The issue of power played a major role in Hagar's story; others had it and she didn't. Power was used to get what was needed out of her.

Then there is the story of Bathsheba. Again, power played a major role in what happened to her. David was king, and the question is *Could she have exercised agency to give consent to his sexual advances or say no?* That's how power works. When unbalanced power dynamics are at play, those being dominated do not have the agency or voice to share what they would like to happen regarding their well-being. That's abuse. Throughout the Bible, we see power being misused and abused to subjugate God's created beings, and this was *not* good in his eyes.

God's Design

The misuse and abuse of power is not what God had in mind when he said in Genesis 1:26, "Let [humankind] have dominion" (PAR). In her book *The Very Good Gospel*, Lisa Sharon Harper writes,

The authors of Genesis 1 could have used as many as eight other words if they had wanted to communicate that dominion means to rule creation in the same way a king rules an empire. But instead, they chose radah, *a primitive root word that means "to tread down or subjugate." It also can mean to rule, but even then it conveys the sense that one rules as the result of winning a struggle.* Radah *is not a call to exercise imperial power. . . . The writers' use of* radah *conjures images of a new creation in need of stewardship.*[6]

When systems are created to dominate people and foster a culture of rape that wreaks havoc in the lives of women and children, this kind of power and control is not of God. They are man-made systems created for those who have a need for deity attributes and not of the Creator God who created everything with goodness and for goodness. And as Harper points out in her book, God created humankind to exercise a different kind of rule from that of kings and empires who rule by oppression.

Genesis directs us to a new order, a new creation where Christ would reign, and his daughters would no longer experience the pain of being subjected or controlled but would live in freedom. Instead of using power to dominate, Jesus humbled himself and submitted himself to the Father's will. This kind of power says that the last shall be first and to lose is to gain (Matthew 19:30; Luke 9:24-25).

Harper goes on to say that "when humanity does not fulfill its call to steward creation, the untamed wilderness takes over. Stewardship requires agency: the use of one's voice to guide and direct and the use of one's mind to make choices that impact the world."[7] In Jesus' order, power and dominion make room for freedom. It makes room for voice and choice, and it doesn't dominate.

It doesn't trample on others to get to the top, and it doesn't abuse to fulfill fleshly and evil desires.

When sexual abuse occurs, I believe the whole creation groans. God weeps. Families are torn apart. Victims are shattered in pieces. Because of that groaning, pain, suffering, and trauma, Jesus emerged. Our Savior, Jesus Christ, came to show the world what true power entails and to offer us salvation. Philippians 2:6-8 (NIrV) says,

> In his very nature he was God.
> > Jesus was equal with God. But Jesus didn't take
> > > advantage of that fact.
> Instead, he made himself nothing.
> > He did this by taking on the nature of a servant.
> > He was made just like human beings.
> He appeared as a man.
> > He was humble and obeyed God completely.
> > He did this even though it led to his death.
> > > Even worse, he died on a cross!

Pathways toward Healing from Sexual Abuse

Jesus has all power; he is equal with God. But we see in his ministry that he didn't use that power to abuse or dominate. Instead, he submitted himself and took the posture of a servant, the lowest position in society, to show that he didn't come to rule like others in positions of power and authority. He came as a servant to save us from oppression, trauma, and all forms of abuse. He came gently and tenderly. He came knowing that we have trust issues. And he offers us freedom, the agency to choose him or not. His strategy of wooing us is extending an invitation and allowing us to respond.

Jesus' posture as a servant offers healing for victims who have been used, abused, and violently forced to comply. Jesus is the primary pathway toward healing, and that pathway began when he came in power, not as the kings of this world, but as a servant who identifies with our pain and suffering and trauma. Jesus came to bring good news and healing for sexual trauma victims. That healing is not only available in Christ but is also attainable through Christ.

The second pathway along this healing journey is learning how to reclaim your voice. To do this level of work, you might need to seek the help of a professional counselor. Sexual abuse takes so much from its victims, including their voices and the emotional resiliency to create boundaries. Part of your healing must come from finding the voice to speak, to scream, to shout yes, to proclaim no, and to dream.

In *I Know Why the Caged Bird Sings*, Maya Angelou writes, "There is no greater agony than bearing an untold story inside you."[8] There is deep pain and sorrow in experiencing something so traumatic without having the voice, the space, or the audience to listen and offer empathy. Part of the recovery process is finding ways to not let shame and debilitating pain have the final word. It is important to tell your story when you want, how you want, to whom you want, and even if you want. So go forth, my sisters, and do the work to heal. Get professional help if you need it. Sexual trauma does not have to be the end of your story. With God's help, you can put the pieces of your life back together. You can create a new life for yourself. Take it one day at a time and one step at a time.

The last pathway on this healing journey involves challenging imbalanced power dynamics in our homes, our communities, and our churches. In Luke 4:18, Jesus said, "The Spirit of the Lord is on me. He has anointed me to announce the good news to poor people. He has sent me to announce freedom for prisoners. He has sent me so that the blind will see again. He wants me to set free those who are treated badly" (NIrv).

We are colaborers with Jesus in the work of announcing the Good News to the oppressed. We are in a partnership with him to announce freedom to those in shackles. And part of our responsibility as those who have found freedom through Jesus Christ is to set others free from abuse and injustice. Our responsibility is to challenge power dynamics that create the atmosphere for abuse in families, communities, and churches. Our responsibility is to speak against imbalanced power dynamics that create unsafe homes for women and children. We are called to use our voices and our power for good and to set captives free, just as Jesus has done. Our job is to advocate for a more just society where power is balanced and we can proclaim, as Paul said in Galatians 3:28 (NIrv), "There is no Jew or Gentile. There is no slave or free person. There is no male or female. That's because you are all one in Christ Jesus." This is gospel-centered balance of power, and that truth will bring about peace and freedom for all in the Kingdom of God.

> Holy God, we call on your name to heal us. You who had
> all power and privilege came in humility and submission
> to show us how the powerful ought to rule. You rule with
> gentleness, kindness, and compassion. And we thank you.
> Thank you for making yourself safe for us to approach and
> have a relationship with. Thank you for giving up your life
> to show us how much you love us and desire our flourishing.
> God, heal us and continue to show us the way to even
> greater healing so that we can stand with those who are
> hurting. In Jesus' name, amen.

QUESTIONS TO EXPLORE

1. How and when did you first learn about sexual abuse?

2. Do you agree that power is a key component of sexual abuse? Why, or why not?

3. List any other biblical people you can think of whose experiences would fit under the category of sexual violence based on the definitions we discussed in this chapter.

4. Where do you see imbalanced power dynamics at work in your family, community, and church?

5. In this chapter, we discussed three pathways toward healing that flow together. How are you doing with your journey toward healing on each of these pathways?

FROM HEAD TO BODY

Safety is often a big priority for abuse survivors. Learning to create safety is vital so that you can access it whenever trauma triggers arise. Another essential component of the healing journey is learning to regulate your emotions.

One of the ways to regulate your emotions is to create a safe and calm space by visualizing a place of safety and calm. Start by visualizing a favorite place that makes you feel safe and joyful. This can be a real place or a fictional place. Think about this place and notice how it looks—its colors, textures, sounds, and even smells. Enter that place, allowing yourself to take it very slowly. This is not a place of chaos that makes you feel dysregulated. This is a place you'd like to go to when the world gets too busy and overwhelming. Describe where you are. What do you see? What do you hear? What do you smell? Notice the temperature. How does it feel? Now feel yourself becoming more and more comfortable there. And take some deep breaths. How does your body feel? Sit in this posture or that place for however long you need to. And take some more deep breaths. When you are ready, take some time to reflect on your experience. Describe your experience and emotions in your journal.

9

ABANDONMENT

This is what the LORD says: . . .
"As a mother comforts her child,
so will I comfort you;
and you will be comforted over Jerusalem."

ISAIAH 66:12-13

The first time I consciously remember meeting my mother and father, I was about ten. That memory will always be frozen in time for me. I still recall the color of the dress my mom was wearing and the type of ensemble my dad had on. In my ten-year-old imagination, they struck me as movie stars. They looked dreamlike, powerful, and beautiful. My mother had on a teal-colored dress with mauve-colored lipstick on her lips and cheeks dusted with blush. With his handsome goatee, Dad was also well dressed in tan-colored pants and a button-down shirt. I was mesmerized in their presence.

They had finally made their way back to Haiti to make good on their promises to bring my three older sisters and me to the US as they had always planned. At this point, they had two other children, my two younger siblings, whose births, I later learned, made it even more possible for all of us to be reunited according to the immigration laws at that time. Preparing for a life where we could live together in peace and with greater opportunities took them more than ten years. Ten years of separation from my parents, with no physical contact. And ten years with no emotional connection. The only form of communication or connection I had with them during those years was infrequent messages on cassette tapes that were sent back and forth through the mail. Though I remember sharing my greetings or whatever else I was told to say on those tapes, I don't remember ever hearing their voices on one of them. So the day we finally met in person was a day of many firsts: the first time I saw my parents face-to-face, the first time I heard their voices, the first time I felt their touch, and the first time we attempted to connect.

I had been told about them for so long that it almost seemed as if I should know them and feel emotionally drawn to them. And yet our reunion, which I assumed was supposed to be a joyous occasion for us to bond, felt distant and disconnected. In that moment of confusion, I hid my little body behind my aunt for protection. When my parents called for me to come to them, I timidly and slowly walked over and managed to crack a polite smile. What was supposed to feel like a warm moment of connection felt cold and scary. I have often wondered if they felt the same emotional distance. At the time, I had no idea that emotional distance would linger for many years. I didn't realize until my adult years that emotional distance had a name or that my feelings were the product of emotional abandonment.

Emotional abandonment is a complex form of trauma that is difficult to accept or believe because the impact isn't easy to see physically or emotionally. Emotional abandonment doesn't always equate to physical neglect. Many families are able to provide for their children's physical needs but not their emotional needs. As a counselor, I've found that those who suffered from emotional abandonment as children have a hard time accepting the diagnosis because their physical needs were often well cared for. How can one, in good conscience, acknowledge emotional abandonment when their physical needs were met? The reality is that those two things can be true at the same time, as was the case in my story. Unlike many families in Haiti, my sisters and I were able to attend quality schools, eat at least one meal a day, and have a roof over our heads because of our parents' sacrifice. At the same time, our emotional needs were severely neglected.

One of the objections I often hear when the subject of emotional abandonment comes up with people in my culture is that it wasn't intentional and that our elders did the best they could. This is a classic case of gaslighting, which invalidates the feelings of those who experienced emotional abandonment and its impact. Emotional abandonment doesn't have to be intentional for it to be traumatic. My parents had a noble reason for leaving Haiti, and I completely understand their reasoning. If I had been in their shoes, given the same circumstances, I probably would have done the same thing. However, realizing this doesn't make the pain of feeling emotionally abandoned any less real. Intent does not determine how the pain is experienced.

The reality is that emotional abandonment often causes its recipients to feel emotionally disconnected and insecure, especially when engaging in relationships. When a child's emotional needs are not met or are inadequately met, it can often lead to all kinds of future relationship challenges. Adults who experienced emotional abandonment as children feel emotionally unequipped and unprepared to manage a big, complex, and scary social world.

In her book *Adult Children of Emotionally Immature Parents*, Lindsay Gibson had this to say about emotional abandonment:

When parents reject or emotionally neglect their children, these children often grow up to expect the same from other people. They lack confidence that others could be interested in them. Instead of asking for what they want, their low self-confidence makes them shy and conflicted about seeking attention. They're convinced they would be bothering others if they tried to make their needs known. Unfortunately, by expecting past rejection to repeat itself, these children end up stifling themselves and promoting more emotional loneliness.[1]

Throughout my life, I have felt the debilitating impact of emotional abandonment. As a people pleaser, I always carried a looming fear of being abandoned and rejected. Whenever conflict arose, I would seek the path of least resistance and try to avoid it. I would approach relationships with my guard up so that others wouldn't hurt me, which often kept me feeling detached and disconnected in relationships. I also developed a hyperindependent façade of not needing help or care from others. Externally I seemed confident and never seemed to be in need of anyone but myself. The thought of ever inconveniencing anyone would sicken me. Of course, this posture made it difficult to be vulnerable and deepen intimacy in many of my relationships.

Attachment Styles

In my quest for understanding the impact of my parents' physical absence for the first ten years of my life, I began researching and asking questions about my story. Through my research, I learned about the different attachment styles and their importance. Diane Poole Heller and other theorists and researchers have done some impactful work around the four core attachment styles. On her website, Heller describes four core attachment styles: secure attachment, avoidant attachment, ambivalent attachment, and disorganized attachment.[2]

Secure Attachment

According to Heller, "Secure attachment is the ideal attachment style needed to enjoy healthy boundaries, fluidity of intimacy, individuation, and social engagement." Children who are securely attached have caregivers who are "positively attuned" to them and "provide a safe haven with consistency and 'good enough' care, attention, and affection." In a safe environment, children feel secure enough to "explore the world [and] interact with others with trust." They also tend to develop emotional resilience and regulation. Securely attached adults "tend to have greater confidence, better balance and choices in relationships, and the ability to both give and receive love." We are hardwired—created by God—for secure attachment. We're subconsciously constantly looking for it. We need safe, consistent, and nurturing relationships.

Avoidant Attachment

Children who develop an avoidant attachment style tend to have caregivers who are "emotionally unavailable, insensitive, rejecting or neglectful to a child's need for connection." So what these children do to cope is disconnect, both physically and emotionally. Think of it this way: It's too painful to daily wait for connection from someone who is unavailable; it's safer and more consistent to disconnect and check out. Remember, we are hardwired for secure attachment. So children and adults with an avoidant attachment style will respond to safe, consistent, and nurturing people.

Ambivalent Attachment

Children with an ambivalent attachment style have caregivers who are inconsistent, or "on-again, off-again." This lack of consistency creates a gamble in the game of connection. *You just never know what you're going to get*, people with this attachment style reason. So what they try to do is look for cues to beat this game, often by adjusting their behaviors to make their parents show up consistently. As adults, they become great at reading the room, ignoring their own needs while still having a "strong desire for connection." They often end up feeling like they're on an emotional high or low from met and unmet needs and therefore are chronically dissatisfied.

Disorganized Attachment

The disorganized attachment style is often identified as the most complex style. Children who develop a disorganized attachment style often have caregivers who send "double-binding messages" or "paradoxical injunctions." Sending a "come here, go away" message creates a no-win situation for a child. An example of a double-binding message is asking a child to sweep the floor and then criticizing the way they do it. Each time the child tries to do it the "right" way, the parent criticizes them and may even punish them.

‡

Honestly, after learning about these attachment styles, I didn't feel enlightened or encouraged to understand the genesis of my broken heart. I felt doomed and broken. I felt that the dysfunctional outcomes I learned about would be my destiny. For the rest of my life, I would be unable to connect with others or make meaningful relationships because my primary connections had been absent. Praise be to God that he's a restorer and is like a mother who comforts her children.

As I dove deeper into investigating how to heal from this kind of trauma, I began to realize that my story wasn't unique. Families all over the world were in situations exactly like mine. Parents had to leave the homes and communities they loved in search of a better life for their families. And everyone involved in these migration shifts experienced unnamed trauma. As children, my siblings and I were often told fanciful stories about our parents being "overseas" in an attempt to pacify our negative feelings and encourage us to accept this reality with honor and pride. I've often heard stories of the many challenges adults have faced on their quest for a better life, but I've rarely heard the children's stories. The reality is that everyone sacrifices something. Children, however, are often not given permission to speak of or feel the pain of abandonment. In God's infinite grace and mercy, the child inside me began to wonder and ask questions about this. She began to feel and discover words to name her feelings, and little by little, she began to heal.

Doing the Healing Work

My healing work began in my early thirties during seminary while I was earning my master's degree in counseling. Each student in this degree program was required to participate in ten counseling sessions. At that time in my life, I had never been to counseling, so I had no idea what to expect. As a therapist, I find it hard to believe that with all the trauma I experienced, I had never once sought out the help of a mental-health professional. All this time, I had been surviving as best as I could without any interventions. In my line of work, I've learned that this is a common story. Most people don't seek professional help unless they're required to do so or their trauma is disrupting their ability to function in life. But many who need the help of a professional counselor don't have the resources, even if the trauma is disrupting their ability to function.

To satisfy the counseling requirement for my degree, I began seeing a therapist in the fall of my second semester in seminary. When I tell you that God is all over the healing journey, I mean it, because the therapist I was assigned was God-sent and hand-picked specifically for me. I called her Ms. Judy until the day she transitioned to eternity. When I first met Ms. Judy, I instantly felt a sense of calm in her presence. When she smiled, it felt genuine and rich with joy. There was nothing fake about her joy. Ms. Judy was a big, tall, beautiful Black woman like the women in my family. Her skin was smooth like milk chocolate.

She would begin each session with the same question: "So, what would you like to discuss today?"

I remember thinking, *I don't know, Ms. Judy. You're the therapist; you tell me.* But I never actually said this out loud.

After developing trust in Ms. Judy, little by little I began telling her my story. Never before had any kind of audience been a witness to my trauma. Never before had I dared to tell another person my story—all of it. And never before had someone stayed present and interested or cared about my feelings. But Ms. Judy created space for me to receive the emotional care I had been needing most of my life.

I remember in one of our sessions, I was emotionally and physically exhausted. I didn't feel like processing my junk. My greatest need at that moment was a nap, not therapy. And right then and there, she gave me permission to rest my eyes and just be. I felt cared for. I felt seen. I felt loved.

Another time, I showed up for therapy bemoaning how life was so difficult and how I just wanted to quit. She let me rant as she always did, and when I was done, she gave me a note that I carried in my wallet for years. It said, "The therapist must survive." It's as if Ms. Judy knew that God had a purpose and a calling on my life, and though I couldn't see it at the time, I needed to survive to be present for it all. Years later we would laugh about those days, and she'd say, "I knew you'd make it." I'm glad she did, because I had no clue.

In one of her final messages to me, she wrote these words:

"Dieula, my heart loves you and cares for your well-being. May God be bigger in your daily affairs than you could ever imagine."

In Isaiah 66:13, God said, "As a mother comforts her child, so will I comfort you." And through Ms. Judy, God did.

I'm fascinated when Scripture refers to God metaphorically as a mother, especially since God is referred to more frequently as a father. It makes me wonder about how modern-day women reflect the qualities of God. Metaphors are used throughout the Bible to help us humans grasp an undefinable God. For example, God is depicted as a potter, or even as an eagle. However, the metaphor of God as a mother causes me to pause the longest because of my early abandonment experiences.

Though both my mother and father left Haiti together, I often find myself more distressed over the absence of my mother during the first ten years of my life. This is partly because the bonding that takes place between a mother and child from the womb is unmatched. And I'm aware that socially, mothers are often designated to care for and nurture their children. I still wonder what a mother-daughter relationship might have felt like if my mother had been present. The truth that I will never experience the nurturing presence of a mother often causes me to grieve. But my heart is restored when I read verses like Isaiah 66:13. It's as if God sees and understands the role a mother plays in a child's emotional growth. And in this verse, God validates the need for comfort in the way a mother comforts her child. Over the years, I have witnessed the hands of God nurturing and comforting me as a mother in ways that have propelled me forward in the healing process.

Hardwired for Relationship

We were created for relationships. From the very beginning God made this fact known, as we see in the account of Creation in

Genesis chapter 1. Everything God put his hands on and created was declared "good" and "very good" (verses 3-31). But there was one thing God said was "not good," and that was "for [humans] to be alone" (2:18). God's intent for us is to be in loving, healthy relationships. As Brené Brown often says, we are hardwired for connection and relationships,[3] and we see proof of that from the very beginning of creation.

The trauma of emotional abandonment can potentially hold us back from experiencing intimacy in our relationships, if we let it. We need to be aware of the impact our primary relationships have on us today. To heal from the trauma of emotional abandonment, we need relationships that can go deep. I'm not referring simply to marital or romantic relationships. I'm talking about all kinds of relationships that allow us to feel known and provide the context to practice setting boundaries. Relationships where we can practice expressing our hurts and anger. Relationships where we can move from people pleasing to a deeper comfort, and where we can risk being vulnerable without fearing the relationship will end. It is in committed relationships that we move toward healing from emotional abandonment. And it is in safe relationships that we can begin to practice the type of intimacy in which God can comfort us like a mother and heal us.

Emotional abandonment and the lack of a secure attachment set the stage for why we need God to mother us, nurture us, comfort us, and heal us so that we can experience secure relationships with the Lord, ourselves, and others. "As a mother comforts her child, so will I comfort you; and you will be comforted" (Isaiah 66:13). What a beautiful promise to be comforted. To be embraced and soothed. Being comforted also implies that something has caused the need for comfort. God knows our pain from emotional abandonment. God is waiting with open arms to embrace us, soothe us, and comfort us. It is in God we find the healing and safety that propel us into secure relationships with others. It is in God we start learning healthy intimacy. It is in God we learn to share our intimate thoughts without the looming fear of abandonment and rejection. It is also in God we learn to be resilient and emotionally strong and not cower in the face of relationship challenges.

> *God, we thank you for offering to nurture us like a mother when our earthly mothers could not. We thank you for always being there, even when we didn't know it. We thank you for being an overwhelming spiritual presence protecting us and preserving us. And we thank you for offering chance after chance to heal through healthy relationships. We pray this in your name, amen.*

QUESTIONS TO EXPLORE

1. What was your emotional care like growing up?

2. Beyond your basic physical needs, did your parents meet your emotional needs? If not, why do you think that was the case?

3. Of the four core attachment styles, which one do you most identify with? What resonates with you with about style?

4. Take some time to assess where you are in your emotional-abandonment healing journey. Do you think the support and healing you currently need are more spiritual, emotional, relational, or therapeutic? Or all these? (Make yourself a note as a reminder to seek the help you've said you need.)

FROM HEAD TO BODY

Expressing gratitude is a great way to shift unpleasant emotions to more pleasant and encouraging ones. It can also help increase sleep and joy.

For this exercise, you will need either a jar or a box. Decorate it to your liking. Then every day, perhaps at the end of the day, write three things that you are grateful for on a slip of paper and put the paper in the jar or box. Your list can include people, places, and things. If you prefer, you can write your list in your journal. Pay attention to your feelings and how your body reacts before and after creating your gratitude list. At the end of the week, review your list for encouragement. If you continue the practice, have one big review at the end of each year.

10

RACIAL TRAUMA

Then the angel of the LORD told [Hagar],
"Go back to your mistress and submit to her."

GENESIS 16:9

After successfully completing another trauma conference in Haiti with my good friends and partners in ministry Betty and Anide, we felt an enormous weight for our sisters there. As we ministered to them, we became aware of structural issues that would persist in the country beyond the conference and continue to impact these women traumatically. We felt the weight of their ongoing trauma and wondered whether the work we had done would have any impact in their healing journeys, especially if they continued to experience this trauma. We cried out to God and questioned where he was as his daughters continually suffered as victims of oppressive systems.

This is the reality of racial trauma. There is a weightiness and weariness when dealing with this form of trauma. From the first European settlements in the 1600s to the present day, the United States has had a brutal four-hundred-year history of enslaving and oppressing Black bodies.[1]

The same legacy of racial trauma is true for other countries in the diaspora, in the Caribbean, in South America, and all over Africa, where the impact of European colonization was felt. It reaches deep into Latin American countries. It goes unnoticed, at times, in Asian communities because of the myth of the model minority. And it has decimated communities and tribes of our Indigenous sisters and brothers. Racism is a structural issue, but its structure is insidious, extending all over the world.

Most people would reject the idea that they are complicit in racism. That has less to do with their individual character and more to do with how racism functions in the modern world. The global impact of Western European and American culture has "centered" white culture to the extent that people of all races often assume it to be superior to other cultures. Non-white cultures and people are assigned value based on how their contributions align with white cultural norms. This takes place on a subconscious level, although it regularly comes to the surface. This culture-wide bent toward "white supremacy" is an idolatrous system we all submit to in implicit and explicit ways until we take intentional steps toward naming it, divesting from it, and healing from it.

As a child of immigrants, I was taught to be blind to racism because I'm from a country governed entirely by Black people. We were taught a watered-down version of our history to forget what truly took place. But one look at modern-day Haiti must cause one to ask, "What happened here?" Certain parts of Haiti look like a crime scene, and it *is* a crime scene in the fight against oppression. For more than three hundred years, the people of Haiti have had to fight for their right to exist as beings created in the image of God. In 1804, Haiti won the fight for its independence from France and became the first Black free nation. And the Haitian people have been paying the price for their freedom ever since. Today, like many cities and corners of the US where Black communities are under-resourced, Haiti is blamed for its own demise. It's a version of victim blaming. That's the impact of historical racial trauma. In the end, the oppressive, traumatic events are no longer discussed or seen as a factor, just the present image standing alone without any historical context. At this point in this book, you should be able to understand why this approach to trauma is misguided.

In this discussion of historical racial trauma, I would be remiss to not address how Black and brown women in America and the diaspora constantly face racial trauma compounded by gender. The intersections where race and gender meet often create a type of trauma that is more complex than unilateral or singular trauma. As Chanequa Walker-Barnes writes, "Intersectionality thus helps us to understand how our experiences of oppression vary based upon our complicated and multilayered identities."[2]

As a Black woman from Haiti and a citizen of the US, I daily feel the weariness of the intersections where my race, ethnicity, and gender meet. As an ordained minister called to preach the Good News, for example, I often feel as though I have no spiritual place to call home. In the Haitian church and many African American churches, my identity as a minister is often marginalized because, according to many of my male counterparts, my gender necessitates that I be silent in the church. And though many predominantly white churches claim to be multiethnic, I often fear attending them, especially when yet another shooting of an unarmed Black person makes the news. Notice I'm referring only to the marginalization I've experienced in what is named the body of Christ. There are countless ways it shows up in the other roles I play.

Many other groups living on the fringes of our society continually face high rates of violence and marginalization and perpetual trauma. To name a few: Indigenous people, especially women and girls; many under the LGBTQIA+ umbrella; trafficked children and women; asylum seekers; and people living in poverty. Typically, wherever there's a minority group in a society, their voice will be hard to hear and understand, their needs will go unnoticed, and they will be even more vulnerable to trauma.

The story of Hagar is yet another example of someone living in a constant state of trauma. Her story in Genesis 16 didn't end with "and she lived happily ever after." We are told in verse 9 that "the angel of the LORD told her, 'Go back to your mistress and submit to her.'"

This is one of those instances when I truly don't understand God. It makes me wonder, *Does God really see?* And it prompts me to ask, *God, what do you mean by telling Hagar to go back and submit to her mistress?*

Trust me, I've heard all the sermons and read many commentaries on this passage, and I still have questions for God. In *Womanist Midrash*, Wilda Gafney writes, "God's message to Hagar is disturbing. She must return to Sarai and submit to her violent and vicious abuse."[3] As a therapist, I would never recommend that someone being abused return to their abuser unless it was their choice. So we are clearly missing some contextual information about this story, because I don't understand how God's instruction is consistent with the message of love we see woven throughout the entire Bible.

I've intentionally highlighted this portion of Hagar's story because this is where we find the tension behind the question "Does God see me?" This is not a question to dance around. Pain and tension with God should be highlighted if we are to understand the grace and love of God. While I don't understand why God would tell Hagar to return to her abusive mistress, I'm okay filing this question under the subject "Things God said in the Bible that I don't understand" rather than creating a whole theological framework around why women should return to their abusers. Or the opposite, which is to write off the Bible and the choice to live a life of dependence on God because they're not relevant to us today. Hagar went back to her mistress as God told her and had to continue fighting for her life and the life of her son. This is what it means to live in a perpetual state of trauma: going back daily and submitting to systems that oppress. Lord, have mercy.

The Impact of Persistent Trauma on Bodies

Persistent trauma not only impacts our feelings; it also breaks down our immune systems, which were designed to help us fight disease and stay alive. Hypertension, heart disease, and diabetes are often found in Black communities, and yet the cause is not simply poor health but health-care disparities and living in persistent trauma without any intervention. This type of trauma weakens the body and keeps it from doing what it was designed to do.

The signs of persistent trauma include the following:

- weariness and fatigue
- hypervigilance (constantly scanning the horizon for danger so we are prepared to defend ourselves)
- the daily reality of being stuck in fight, flight, or freeze mode
- heightened levels of fear for ourselves and our loved ones
- life adjustments to ensure safety and survival
- anxiety, depression, suicidal ideation, physical symptoms of pain, chronic hypertension, and heart issues
- pent-up aggression
- numbness

- hopelessness
- distrust
- death

Yes, death is a real response to racial trauma. For example: On October 12, 2019, a Fort Worth police officer shot and killed twenty-eight-year-old Atatiana Jefferson while she was playing video games with her eight-year-old nephew.[4] On November 9, 2019, Marquis Jefferson, the father of Atatiana, died suddenly at the age of fifty-nine of what many believed to be a broken heart.[5] On January 9, 2020, Yolanda Carr, the mother of Atatiana, died at the age of fifty-five—again, of what many said was a broken heart.[6] And on January 30, 2023, Amber Carr, the sister of Atatiana, died at the age of thirty-three.[7] Racial trauma often has a ripple effect on the entire community.

Of course, these tragic responses to living in persistent trauma make complete sense. Racial trauma can have a significant impact on its victims as they try to navigate multiple emotions, where happiness often competes with a sense that trouble is just around the corner. Not only is racism pervasive around the world, but so are anti-Blackness and white supremacy. I'm frequently shocked when I see racism and anti-Blackness around the world because I expect other marginalized groups of color to know better and take better care of others who are oppressed. I often feel that there is no true place to simply rest and be fully human here on earth. I also tend to forget that we are dealing with forces and principalities of the evil one, and his end game is world dominion.

These are the questions that confront us: How do we help those living with persistent trauma find a path toward healing and restoration? Can the human soul survive, and dare I say thrive, in a perpetual state of trauma?

A Holistic Approach to Healing from Racial Trauma

Until Christ returns to overcome the evil systems of the world, bringing about the new heaven and the new earth, racial disparities and trauma are issues we will grapple with. This reality often creates a sense of hopelessness and helplessness for me, but I'm reminded that God invites us to join him in dismantling these systems. Through the power of the Holy Spirit, we can step forth and create a more just world where all of God's created beings can flourish. To do that, a holistic approach to healing from racial trauma is necessary.

Prayer

Healing for those who live in perpetual trauma should always begin with prayer. Social movements that take a stand against deeply rooted societal structures have no chance of succeeding without prayer. Prayer is the anchor that keeps us steady and reminds us that "our struggle is not against flesh and blood, but against the rulers, against the authorities, against the powers of this dark world and against the spiritual forces of evil in the heavenly realms" (Ephesians 6:12). When we pray, we engage with the Holy Spirit, who fights with us and for us. Prayer helps us keep the faith as we see evil prospering. Prayer helps us stay committed, encouraged, and connected to one another in the community for the long haul. And prayer fuels the energy needed to fight for justice in an unjust world.

Fighting for Equity

Fighting for equitable practices in society is an important component of any initiative that seeks to heal racial trauma. As we do the emotional work in this healing journey, we must also do the physical work of addressing and removing the sources that are producing the trauma. The emotional and physical go hand in hand. Justice is about doing what is right by ensuring that vulnerable populations are seen, represented, supported, and given every opportunity to flourish. Isaiah 58:6-7 says,

> *"Is not this the kind of fasting I have chosen:*
> *to loose the chains of injustice*
> *and untie the cords of the yoke,*
> *to set the oppressed free*
> *and break every yoke?*
> *Is it not to share your food with the hungry*
> *and to provide the poor wanderer with shelter—*
> *when you see the naked, to clothe them,*
> *and not to turn away from your own flesh and blood?"*

In Luke 4, Jesus quoted the same passage from Isaiah to remind us that he came to ensure that justice is served and to set the oppressed free. This is our task as well. We are called to work toward the defeat of racial trauma that impacts God's created beings and prevents them from flourishing. We must be well acquainted with advocacy work, and we must use our voices, our influence, our finances, and our power to ensure that all people are free from the oppression of racial injustice. Though we may not see it in our lifetimes, we must continue to join God in his work of setting free the oppressed, traumatized, and vulnerable.

Trauma-Informed Counseling

As we pray and fight for justice and equality, we must prioritize trauma-informed care for those who suffer from persistent trauma. To ensure that victims have a chance at living productive lives beyond the constant struggle to survive, we must create an awareness of the need for robust counseling and healing groups.

Institutions and churches, in particular, need to become trauma-informed spaces. As society becomes more vocal about mental-health needs, the church has a great opportunity to meet the need for racial-trauma healing among its BIPOC sisters. (*BIPOC* stands for "Black, Indigenous, and people of color.") It is important for leaders of churches and organizations to understand the pervasiveness and persistence of racial trauma and find ways to become places of safety that foster healing. Counseling and healing groups for the racially traumatized are not just a luxury for the privileged and the elite; they are a necessity for the under-resourced as well.

I believe people of European descent also need racial trauma–informed counseling. I remember looking at an image of a lynching from the internet in which men, women, and children were all gathered around a body hanging from a tree as they were picnicking. As a trauma therapist, I often wonder what that normalized trauma did to that community. Did any of the children have trauma responses? No one can absorb witnessing and/or experiencing hundreds of years of trauma throughout generations without any form of intentional trauma healing and remain okay. Healing for our sisters and brothers of European descent must include awareness, lamenting, repentance, divesting from racist systems, forgiveness, and reparation.[8]

Self-Care

We also need to reimagine what overall wellness and self-care can look like in BIPOC communities that are facing persistent racial trauma. I love the words of Chichi Agorom in *The Enneagram for Black Liberation*: "We are not here to just fight and suffer until we die. We get to choose rest, ease, and joy for ourselves."[9] Yes, we must fight for justice, but we must also create spaces for joy.

For the racially traumatized, self-care must be a priority that every church and institution champions and encourages. We can't simply think of self-care as an individual practice to improve the self in isolation; we must embrace care for the traumatized in the context of loving communities. Chichi Agorom says, "What we know to be true, however, is that our wellness and liberation do not exist separate from the collective."[10] Self-care and wellness in a vacuum are sure ways to perpetuate burnout and loneliness. A holistic approach to self-care will embrace engaging with the community, sharing your needs, and having the community show up to celebrate and reinforce your need for care. Self-care challenges the status quo, and it helps with playing the long game in life that reaches beyond survival. So take deep breaths, go on long walks, dance, turn off the news, meet up with friends, create loving circles where you can be fully present, and allow your soul to rest. And do these things often to survive and—dare I say—thrive.

Awareness and Self-Love

Racial-trauma healing has been a continual journey for me that began with an awareness in college that led me to take many Africana-studies courses. This is where I started to understand the history of my own people in Haiti, the fight for freedom in South Africa during apartheid, and the history of the enslaved in the US. I wanted to understand what I was seeing and feeling in America. As my understanding grew, I went through a season of deep lament and grief.

My parents were very proud Haitians who loved their country. They'd listen to Haitian radio stations for news, they played the music that is often seen as sacrilegious in many Christian circles, and my dad frequently traveled back and forth to Haiti. Their plan was always to return to Haiti and retire there. Their pride in Haiti made me even more proud of being Black. Which made the next step of my trauma-healing journey an important one. In the twenty-two years I had lived in the US, I had never returned to Haiti for a visit, partly because everyone had warned me that it was too dangerous. But after attending seminary, I decided to return.

My trip back to Haiti was a beautiful gift I didn't know I needed. I cried the entire journey. When I saw a little girl who was exactly my age when I left, I couldn't contain the tears. For the first time, I saw a version of myself that I had tucked away for twenty-two years. In Haiti, I fell in love with Blackness again. I fell in love with myself again. It was on that trip to Haiti that God changed the trajectory of my life. He gave me a new purpose that would lead me to serve hurting sisters around the world.

This was my first sankofa trip. *Sankofa* is a word from the Akan people in Ghana, West Africa, that means "to go back and retrieve what is at risk of being lost." A part of me was at risk of being lost, and I had to go back and retrieve it. And the process of retrieving it set me on a path I would follow for the rest of my life.

Another sankofa journey for me was joining a mixed-race-and-gender group of pastors on a chartered bus to Tennessee, Alabama, and Mississippi. We walked the bridge in Selma, Alabama, and remembered Bloody Sunday. Then we visited the church where four little girls were murdered on a Sunday right before service began. But the part of the trip that still causes me to question how humans can stray so far from the heart of God was visiting the lynching memorial in Montgomery, Alabama. Developed by the Equal Justice Initiative with the oversight of director Bryan Stevenson, the National Memorial for Peace and Justice had a deep impact on me. I will never forget the shock, grief, and sadness I felt that day. The memorial was created as a reminder that we must confront the legacy of racial terror. Remembering helps us confront the truth of evil. Remembering cautions our souls to never get comfortable with injustice toward anyone anywhere. I had to go back and retrieve courage from those who fought for freedom and continue on the quest for shalom.

These sankofa journeys were building blocks for the ultimate journey that connected the dots for me: my trip to the African nations of Benin and Nigeria. After a series of events rediscovering my maternal family tree and learning of my ancestry from Benin and Nigeria through DNA testing, I traveled there to retrieve something else I had lost. I will never forget how it felt being in a country where I was surrounded by Black people. Instantly, my racial defenses came down. I wasn't hyperaware of my skin color or afraid of being hypervisible and invisible at the same time. I just breathed and allowed myself to take it all in.

The most impactful part of this journey was walking the same path my ancestors had walked in chains before taking a final look at the land they called home and boarding ships to the point of no return on the Atlantic Ocean. I sat on the sandy beach, closed my eyes, and just listened to the waves. This moment was filled with so many unnamed emotions that my body expressed tears to capture them all. At some point, I mumbled "Thank you" to my ancestors. Being so near the ocean felt like a return of sorts, as though they had returned home through me. My presence served as a witness to their trauma and survival. I owed them a thank you.

Racial-trauma healing will look different for each of us. Only you can name what's been taken from you and what needs to be reclaimed. I pray that as you continue this journey of healing, God will be with you every step of the way. I also pray that you will trust God to guide you to safe healing spaces and people and sankofa journeys that will show you how to live more and more into the fullness of who you are until he returns.

Creator God, we believe your Word when it says you created humans "very good." Help us live into the goodness that you say we have. Help us flourish as your beings created in your image. Give us the boldness to fight for justice and the courage to admit we are tired. Lead us into rest, joy, and peace until you return. Amen.

QUESTIONS TO EXPLORE

1. If you have been living in a perpetual state of trauma, what is your unique situation?

2. What has living in perpetual trauma been like for you?

3. How have you managed balancing the fight for justice with your wellness and self-care?

4. Where do you find rest? Safe healing spaces? Safe people?

5. What does self-care look like for you?

6. In what ways are you growing spiritually in spite of persistent trauma?

FROM HEAD TO BODY

Somatic work is a powerful resource in the trauma-healing journey. Author and psychotherapist Resmaa Menakem says that "the practices of Somatic Abolitionism are not strategies, tactics, tools, or weapons. They are bodily experiences. That's why, as you'll see, most of them involve moving, touching, holding, releasing, protecting, weeping, laughing, singing, or the cultivation of joy."[11]

For this exercise, you'll use one of Menakem's body practices to help you free the trauma that resides in your body.

Find a quiet, private, comfortable place. Sit down. Put one hand on your knee or in your lap. Place the other on your belly.

Now hum. Not from your throat or chest, but from the bottom of your belly.

Hum strong and steady. Push the air out of your belly firmly, not gently.

Stop to breathe in, but return to the hum with each new breath.

Experience the hum in your belly. Then sense it in the rest of your body.

Continue humming for two minutes.

When you're done, reach your arms upward. Then, slowly and gently, feel your body with your hands, starting from the top of your head. Move slowly down your neck and along your chest, then below your waist, then past your knees, until your arms are fully extended downward. What do you notice?[12]

PART THREE

FINDING FREEDOM FROM YOUR TRAUMA STORY

11

TELLING YOUR STORY

The angel of the LORD found Hagar near a spring in the desert; it was the spring that is beside the road to Shur. And he said, "Hagar, slave of Sarai, where have you come from, and where are you going?"

GENESIS 16:7-8

In 2004, we uprooted our family from New Jersey and moved to the Dallas area so I could work on my master's degree in counseling. Everything in Texas felt foreign. I was hundreds of miles from my Haitian community. The climate and the culture were a shock, and even the people's "southern charm" was hard to get used to. I stood out quite significantly. My East-Coast-with-a-blend-of-Caribbean accent was a dead giveaway that I was new to the area.

The questions would most often come from church members:

"What's your story?"

"Where are you from?"

"How'd you get here from Haiti?"

I was unprepared for the invasiveness of their questions and often felt like a fish in a fishbowl. I seemed to fascinate people, who constantly asked more questions that left me feeling exhausted.

Questions that others might consider friendly often tend to throw off people who have experienced trauma. We are blindsided at first, but then we begin to strategize for the next invasion. To do that, we come up with safe answers that won't trigger us or leave us exhausted and will keep us in control without sharing more than we desire.

One of my safe answers usually goes something like this: "I was born in Haiti, grew up in New Jersey, and spent years living in Texas with my family." In one sentence, I give them the beginning, middle, and current end of the story. When I'm really tired and want people to back off, I simply respond, "I'm from New Jersey." It's a boring state that no one ever dares to ask any follow-up questions about. Sorry, Jerseyans.

Telling your story honestly and authentically when you're ready can set you free and inspire others. However, if you tell your story when you're not ready, it can leave you feeling exposed, desperately desiring to hide because you shared too much too deeply with people who are ill equipped to handle your emotions.

The Samaritan Woman

In John 4:7-9, we see the beginning of a beautiful conversation between Jesus and a woman he met at a well in the region of Samaria.

> When a Samaritan woman came to draw water, Jesus said to her, "Will you give me a drink?" (His disciples had gone into the town to buy food.)
> The Samaritan woman said to him, "You are a Jew and I am a Samaritan woman. How can you ask me for a drink?" (For Jews do not associate with Samaritans.)

In these verses, Jesus and the Samaritan woman revealed deeper truths about themselves to each other. It was a mutual sharing and a mutual seeing. Their interaction began with Jesus' posture toward the Samaritan woman and a peculiar question: "Will you give me a drink?" It was a question Jesus knew would elicit the response she gave. A question he knew for sure would disarm her so he could enter into her life and set her free.

The Samaritan woman was fetching water in the middle of the day, which is a dead giveaway that something was wrong. This portion of her story always reminds me that we, in the modern world with running water from our kitchen faucets, were not the original audience for this narrative; if we were, we would instantly understand why this woman's behavior was odd and possibly a trauma response. The women I've taught in Haiti, Uganda, Kenya, and Congo understand that most women with a local well would fetch water in the morning to prepare for their daily chores and beat the scorching sun later in the day. A well was a place that drew people together. Friends would meet, conversations would take place, and local news and gossip would be spread. Why would this woman not want to connect with her community? Perhaps she was an introvert and wanted to be by herself. I've heard this response before.

If you read further in her story, Jesus exposed something about her that revealed him as a prophet. He said to the woman, "The fact is, you have had five husbands, and the man you now have is not your husband" (verse 18).

Let's be honest: A woman married five times raises eyebrows in the modern world; but in the ancient world, where morality and customs weren't as free, it would have been scandalous. In light of this fact, it makes sense that she would fetch water in the middle of the day. This woman was more than likely hiding in shame.

According to customs in her day, as a woman, it was almost

impossible for her to petition for divorce, since she was legally bound to her husband forever. This meant that her previous five husbands might have initiated a divorce and abandoned her. Or they could have died. Either way, she was a traumatized woman in need of Jesus to breathe new life into her and set her free.

Jesus' posture toward the traumatized was gentle, kind, patient, and compassionate. He was never intrusive or shaming. His interaction with the Samaritan woman was similar to the one Hagar had with God in the desert, where she not only felt that God had seen her, but she also saw God in a whole new way. That mutual seeing set both women free in a way that comforted them. Both of their interactions with God began with a question—not just any kind of question, but a question that made them feel seen and known.

Guidance for Telling Your Story

This part of the book will help you prepare to tell your story if that's what you'd like to do. You may start by telling your story to yourself and then discern whether you'd like to share it with others. You also need to discern who has earned the right to hear your story, since not everyone has earned it. The questions that follow will help you work through either one of those steps.

But first a few words of wisdom: Keep in mind that everyone is at a different place in their trauma-healing journey. Someone with a traumatic past like yours may be open and ready to share their story, but that may not be how you'd like to proceed in your own healing journey. Both of you are free to proceed however you choose.

You may never want to share certain parts of your trauma story publicly, and that is completely fine too. It doesn't mean you're any less healed. Sometimes less is more. Using your boundaries is a sign that healing is taking place.

If you're working through your trauma narrative with a counselor and don't want to do this exercise, that is completely fine as well. You can skip this part entirely if you prefer. This is a no-pressure process.

For those of you who would like to share your trauma story with others one-on-one or in a small group, here are some additional words of wisdom to guide you: You don't have to share your story with everyone you meet to prove you're healed. You should never feel forced or manipulated into sharing your story. Telling others your story should be your decision as you do the healing work. Be sure you've established trust and safety with those who will be hearing your story. Ideally, you'll have established a connection with them over a period of time. Take deep breaths and take your time, pausing or completely stopping if you feel uncomfortable. This is an opportunity to practice good self-care before, during, and after.

Use the following questions as a guide to help you tell your trauma story:

- What happened to you? (See if you can share your story in just a few sentences.)
- What meaning did you make out of what happened to you?
- How did it leave you feeling?
- What did you say about yourself after the trauma?
- How do you think others saw you after the trauma?
- How do you think God saw you after the trauma?
- What were your thoughts toward God after the trauma?
- What has been the hardest part of your trauma story to work through?

- What parts of your story are still hard for you?
- What lies have you believed about yourself because of the trauma?
- Are there any truths you're trying to claim or have claimed about yourself? Write them down.
- What Scripture has been a constant source of strength for you throughout this healing journey?
- What glimpses of hope have you found throughout your healing journey?
- What sources of joy have you discovered throughout the healing journey?

As you share your story, I pray that those who hear it will have the posture Jesus showed toward those in need—a posture of gentleness, kindness, patience, and compassion. I hope their posture will communicate that they are present with you and actively listening. I pray it may leave you feeling seen and known rather than exposed.

God, we can't always make sense of why trauma is a part of our world. We can't understand why we experience pain and suffering in our lives, but we believe that you are a good God and that you wept for and with each of us through our trauma. You identify with us in a way that lets us know we were not alone. Thank you for giving us the strength to take this step of telling our stories, naming the pain, and giving ourselves new opportunities in life. Continue to be near us. In your compassionate name, amen.

QUESTIONS TO EXPLORE

1. What has kept you from sharing your trauma story with others? What anxieties or fears do you have about sharing your story?

2. How did you respond to the conversation between Jesus and the Samaritan woman? What stood out to you about Jesus' posture toward her?

3. If you feel ready to share your story, whom will you share it with and in what context?

4. If you've already shared your story for the first time, how did it make you feel?

FROM HEAD TO BODY

In Black diasporic churches, movement is a central part of worship. I'd like to think our ancestors knew a thing or two about the interconnectedness of our bodies and brains because they left us with expressions of dance and movement to heal our trauma.

Movement sends messages to your brain that can help shift your energy and boost your mood. Moving your body can also help you fight against anxiety, depression, intrusive thoughts, and stress. This is why I applaud all the expressions of dance and movement that people in the Black diaspora have created.

For this exercise, I recommend moving your body in any rhythmic, playful, or athletic manner that feels comfortable to you. This can include walking, jumping up and down, dancing, clapping, jogging in place, or just stretching. As you move, focus on how your body is feeling in the moment. Pay attention to your feelings before and after moving your body.

12

LAMENTING YOUR TRAUMA STORY

*Lament challenges the church to acknowledge real
suffering and plead with God for his intervention. . . .
Lament is honesty before God and each other.*

SOONG-CHAN RAH,
Prophetic Lament

We need to name a tension that often makes the process of healing from trauma even more challenging. That tension relates to
two key questions: Where was God when our trauma occurred?
And why didn't he prevent the trauma? My attempts at responding to these questions will more than likely be insufficient for
your specific situation. I have read many theological discussions
on the subject, and the answers were often insufficient for me,
too, especially amid my own pain. In fact, one thing that angers
me the most is the simplistic answers people give in an attempt to
resolve theological tensions that are too complex for our limited

understanding to grasp. So my hope for this chapter is not to give definitive answers to these questions but to name the tension that trauma survivors often experience, give you permission to wrestle with God, and provide the space for you to simply lament and cry out to God.

In seminary, I remember studying about the prophet Habakkuk, who bellowed a profound lament to God, accusing him of not listening to his cries for help:

> How long, LORD, must I call for help,
>   but you do not listen?
> Or cry out to you, "Violence!"
>   but you do not save?
> Why do you make me look at injustice?
>   Why do you tolerate wrongdoing?
> Destruction and violence are before me;
>   there is strife, and conflict abounds.
>
> HABAKKUK 1:2-3

These verses seemed distant to me in seminary. American academia tends to sanitize the raw voices of suffering throughout the Bible. It was hard for me to understand Habakkuk's context and the magnitude of his pain when everyone around me seemed to be living a victorious Christian life. There appeared to be no room to ask difficult questions about God's seeming aloofness to pain. It wasn't until years later that I started wrestling with my own pain and the pain of this world, which led me to ask God some serious questions like these: *How long do we need to keep crying out "There's violence in the streets and our homes" until you listen? How long must we keep looking at injustice and bodies in the streets? Why do you do absolutely nothing about violence and wrongdoing, oh God?*

Ouch! If you were taught to never question God, you may be

squirming in your seat right now. You may even be ready to defend God. But sit with the tension for just a second.

A while back, I wrote these lamenting thoughts in my journal as I sought to understand the ways of God:

> I had a great conversation about you today, and the question of your presence when there's pain and suffering came up. To be honest, I don't know or understand. I believe in your sovereignty, that you're all-knowing and powerful. And I believe you are always near and present. I don't understand why you don't prevent pain and suffering or completely end it today once and for all. I don't believe you're the one orchestrating evil in this world because an evil God could not create such beauty—the earth, the moon, the stars, and such beautiful people. So if you're all-knowing and you're not evil, yet at the same time you do not prevent pain and suffering, then what is going on here? I don't understand. I know my understanding is limited, but I'm struggling.

I've realized that the back-and-forth questioning of God's posture in the presence of pain and trauma is not only a common part of the spiritual journey; it's also one of the most necessary and expected ways to engage a relational God when we're suffering.

You Are Not Alone

One of the most eye-opening revelations I experienced during my season of questioning was realizing that I wasn't alone. That revelation shifted my posture toward God. I had regular conversations with two friends who had suffered trauma and tragic losses, and their validation of my anger, disappointment, and doubts normalized my experiences of wrestling with God. We spent countless hours discussing the depth of our pain, doubt, and confusion while remaining committed to following Christ.

During one of our conversations, I realized that many facets of God didn't seem to add up, and I couldn't understand it. With sadness I said to them, "If I walked away from God, where else would I go?" They nodded as if we all shared that thought at some point in our lives.

I also began to read literature about different authors in the faith who wrestled with God and doubted in similar ways. Authors like Renita Weems, who wrote the book *Listening for God*; Austin Channing Brown, who wrote *I'm Still Here*; Barbara Brown Taylor, who wrote *Learning to Walk in the Dark*; and even Mother Teresa. That community of wrestlers gave me the language to wrestle with God while being confident that he would be found somewhere in the wrestling. It's not unusual for those who are suffering to look to God for comfort and, at the same time, accuse him of not preventing pain.

Perhaps, when Jesus cried from the cross that God had abandoned him, he was modeling for us a relationship with God that can handle our disappointments, doubts, and accusations. Throughout the Bible, we see a persecuted group of God's people who often cried out to God for deliverance. Not only did they learn to sit in the tension of God not showing up in the way they anticipated, but they also learned ways to engage him in the tension.

As an ordained minister, I have many rehearsed theological responses when questions arise about God's posture in the presence of pain and suffering. I know to point people to passages like Isaiah 55:8-9: "'My thoughts are not your thoughts, neither are your ways my ways,' declares the LORD. 'As the heavens are higher than the earth, so are my ways higher than your ways and my thoughts than your thoughts.'" But offering theological answers and comforting Scriptures can hurt more than it helps. This is why I always recommend using wisdom and discernment in applying biblical apologetics to support a person reeling from trauma.

The Posture of Lament

The theological and biblical posture of lament is an appropriate posture in and of itself, and Christians don't talk about it enough. I would argue that part of our healing comes from lament and crying out to God about the pain. Soong-Chan Rah writes, "Lament in the Bible is a liturgical response to the reality of suffering and engages God in the context of pain and trouble. The hope of lament is that God would respond to human suffering that is wholeheartedly communicated through lament."[1]

When I was growing up in Haiti, the women and men of the church would gather once a week as a community for prayer. They'd walk together to one of the nearby mountains and place themselves inside the rock crevices, where they would spend hours in lament. They'd sing a solemn song and then cry out to God with wailing prayers about the suffering they were facing. After hours of lamenting and praying, they would find new strength to persevere. Lament is not about drumming up impeccable, one-size-fits-all answers or pretending that there is no tension. And it isn't about dismissing the fact that we don't always understand the ways of God. Lament is about leaning into the tension and borrowing the language of lament from the Psalms to engage God.

The most appropriate, biblical, and theological thing we can do as we wrestle with God over his silent posture when we're facing pain is this: engage him in it through lament. Let's do that now.

Almighty God, I lift up the pain and suffering of my sisters and brothers today. Hear their voices crying out for your comfort and protection.

For those who have suffered the pain of abandonment and neglect—God, hear our prayers and give us the strength to hold on, to heal, and to persevere.

For those who have suffered the pain and trauma of childhood sexual abuse—God, hear our prayers and give us the strength to hold on, to heal, and to persevere.

For those who have suffered the pain and trauma of domestic violence—God, hear our prayers and give us the strength to hold on, to heal, and to persevere.

For those who have suffered the pain of divorce—God, hear our prayers and give us the strength to hold on, to heal, and to persevere.

For those who are overwhelmed by the grief of losing a child—God, hear our prayers and give us the strength to hold on, to heal, and to persevere.

For those who are grieving the loss of a parent, sibling, or spouse—God, hear our prayers and give us the strength to hold on, to heal, and to persevere.

For those who are homeless with not enough to eat—God, hear our prayers and give us the strength to hold on, to heal, and to persevere.

For those who are constantly navigating racial trauma—God, hear our prayers and give us the strength to hold on, to heal, and to persevere.

For those who are navigating migration, immigration, and survival in a new land—God, hear our prayers and give us the strength to hold on, to heal, and to persevere.

For those who have been overlooked, underestimated, unseen, and denigrated—God, hear our prayers and give us the strength to hold on, to heal, and to persevere.

For those navigating cultural shame—God, hear our prayers and give us the strength to hold on, to heal, and to persevere.

For those who have suffered discrimination because of their gender—God, hear our prayers and give us the strength to hold on, to heal, and to persevere.

For those who have suffered verbal abuse and terror from

those whom they loved—God, hear our prayers and give us the strength to hold on, to heal, and to persevere.

For those who feel they are often second-class citizens in their homes, without a voice or power or equality—God, hear our prayers and give us the strength to hold on, to heal, and to persevere.

For those who have been sold, trafficked, and prostituted—God, hear our prayers and give us the strength to hold on, to heal, and to persevere.

For those who were left to die—God, hear our prayers and give us the strength to hold on, to heal, and to persevere.

For those who have suffered religious abuse—God, hear our prayers and give us the strength to hold on, to heal, and to persevere.

For all the pain and trauma . . .

God, hear our prayers and give us the strength to hold on, to heal, and to persevere.

God, we thank you for hearing our prayers. Amen.

QUESTIONS TO EXPLORE

1. Has it ever seemed like God let you down? How did you feel when that happened?

2. What difficult questions have you asked God? Have you ever cried out in lament to God and wrestled with him in your pain? What was this experience like for you?

3. How do you feel hearing others share openly about their disappointment in God?

4. Did you ever get back into a good relationship with God? If so, what was your process?

FROM HEAD TO BODY

In this chapter, we practiced lamenting verbally. Now I want you to allow your body to lament physically.

Kneel on a yoga mat, towel, or blanket.

Then lean forward, resting your butt on your heels and your forehead on the floor. Move your arms so they're next to your legs, with your palms facing up. Inhale and exhale, slowly and deeply, for at least eight breaths.

In this pose, let your body release your deep lament. Allow yourself to cry as you stretch and breathe.

Notice how you feel as you lament. Write your observations and feelings in your journal.

13

FORGIVING OTHERS

"And you, my child, will be called a prophet of the Most High;
for you will go on before the Lord to prepare the way for him,
to give his people the knowledge of salvation
through the forgiveness of their sins,
because of the tender mercy of our God,
by which the rising sun will come to us from heaven
to shine on those living in darkness
and in the shadow of death,
to guide our feet into the path of peace."

LUKE 1:76-79

I came to faith when I was around ten years old. I remember the sermon like it was yesterday, because it scared me to death. My sisters and I were living in the capital of Haiti, Port-au-Prince, with our uncle and his family, awaiting our visas to enter the US, so we weren't in our familiar surroundings. The community was different, much more modern than we were accustomed to.

Church in the capital was different too. On the Sunday I accepted Christ, I was wearing a borrowed dress and shoes from one of my older cousins, Rose. The church was small, with a corrugated tin roof and walls made with tarps. It was the end of a revival series, so the church service was full and lively that Sunday. The guest preacher was a Haitian man from the US. His persuasive sermon encouraged us to put our faith in Jesus Christ for the forgiveness of our sins. But the part of the sermon that scared me was when the preacher looked me dead in my eye (or so it seemed) and said, "If you don't put your faith in Jesus Christ and repent and ask God for forgiveness, the Communist Party will take over the country, and you will die and be sent to hell." Now do you understand the fear I felt as I ran back to my uncle's house and prayed a prayer asking Jesus to come into my heart?

I can't help but chuckle as I think of that small child running home in the heat of the day to pray that God would forgive her. Now I know that God is more gracious and loving than that preacher made him out to be. There's no need to use fear tactics or manipulation to persuade people to accept Christ. His reputation is enough to woo people into a relationship with him. Nonetheless, I embrace the profound significance of submitting, even as a child, to a loving and faithful relationship with Christ. I am reminded that every day all over the world, people come to faith in Christ in many different ways—sometimes as a result of hearing a loving gospel message, and other times out of fear of spending eternity in hell. My hope is that all who come to faith will understand and accept the process of reconciliation with God through the life, death, and resurrection of Jesus.

God offered us forgiveness through the sacrifice of Jesus Christ. And to partake in this free gift of forgiveness, reconciliation, and eternal life with him, one must accept it by faith, repenting of sin, renouncing it as our lord, embracing a new life in Christ, and making him our Lord. Second Corinthians 5:17 says, "If anyone is in Christ, the new creation has come: The old has gone, the new is here!" Part of the process of being reconciled to God and becoming new creations in Christ is renouncing ties to our old patterns of living and accepting a new reality.

We can't commit our lives to Christ and walk away from the subject of forgiveness. Forgiveness is a big deal, and to understand how to forgive others, we must begin with Christ and the forgiveness he modeled for us. I often feel a tension in Christian communities around this topic. When Christ is brought up in conversations on forgiveness, it is often done to guilt others into forgiving before they are ready. I hope I've demonstrated throughout this book that Christ is patient with us as we are healing. Guilt should never be used to move us toward forgiveness.

To be forgiven and reconciled to God requires confession, repentance, and a commitment to live rightly and justly before God. This is the only path to enjoying the fruits of a relationship with him.

Whether we are conscious of it or not, this is a lifelong process of transformation. Because we are fallen human beings who are prone to wander and fail, we must repeat this process of confession, repentance, and commitment to righteousness over and over again. We don't need it for salvation but rather to make us more like Christ our Savior.

I can testify that over the years, this process has transformed not only who I am but also how I live day to day.

Forgiving Others

From the work I've done as a counselor, I can say with certainty that the healing journey almost never begins with forgiveness. Forgiveness is often sprinkled throughout the journey, but it's rarely the first step. In the beginning, most people cannot see a way to ever forgive the person who committed an offense against them. It's not uncommon for me to have clients who request my counseling services because they would like to forgive someone who has caused them harm, and they're having a hard time doing so. My strategy with them resembles what I've laid out in this book. We work through the trauma they've experienced before processing the forgiveness part of the trauma-healing journey.

Forgiving the person who has caused your trauma is one of the top three most difficult things to do on the healing journey. The reason why it's so difficult is that we tend to treat forgiveness as a one-size-fits-every-situation process. That is the wrong approach. We must approach forgiveness on a case-by-case basis because the situation will dictate how to best handle the process. To forgive others, we need to cultivate wisdom and acceptance.

The Need for Wisdom

In the book *How the Bible Actually Works*, Peter Enns considers Proverbs 26:4-5, two proverbs that seems to give competing instructions, as an exercise in how to handle complex situational issues from a biblical perspective:

> These two clearly contradictory proverbs aren't a problem that needs fixing. The biblical writers weren't idiots. Placing these two opposite sayings side by side gives us a snapshot of how wisdom works. . . . Both of these sayings are wise, and the one we act upon here and now, at this unscripted moment, depends on which fits the current situation best. Reading the situation—not simply the Bible—is what wisdom is all about. It's also, as we'll see, what the life of faith is about.[1]

Yes, the Bible is clear in its instructions about forgiveness, but we also need to rely on wisdom to help us navigate forgiving others, especially the offenders who caused our trauma. James 1:5 says, "If any of you lacks wisdom, you should ask God, who gives generously to all without finding fault, and it will be given to you." And as Enns points out, "Seeking wisdom rather than grabbing for answers is what this life of faith is about."[2]

The Need for Acceptance

Throughout my own journey of forgiveness, I've paid attention to the language different trauma survivors use to describe their own forgiveness journeys. In her book *The Wisdom of Sundays*, Oprah Winfrey notes that "'forgiveness is giving up the hope that the past could be any different,' . . . accepting the past for what it was, and using this moment and this time to help yourself move forward."[3]

The key word here is *acceptance*. We need to accept the past for what it was and the fact that we cannot change how events played out. At the same time, we still accept that those events and the person or persons responsible for them were wrong. When I've come to terms with the reality of what happened and distance myself from it, I am then free to let go of the need for revenge against the person or groups of people who have harmed me. Forgiveness is about changing the relationship we have with the wrong that's been done to us. However, arriving at that place is a process.

Victims of trauma often have objections to forgiving because they believe forgiveness means the following:

- If I forgive, I'm saying the wrong was okay.
- If I forgive, I'm giving the offender permission to harm me again.
- If I forgive, the offender will get away with what they did to me.
- If I forgive, the offender will see me as a weak person.
- If I forgive, the offender will never change.
- If I forgive, I will have to reconcile with the offender.

What personal objection would you add to this list?

A while ago, I stumbled upon a dear friend's Substack newsletter. Sharifa Stevens has penned some of the most beautiful words regarding her struggles to forgive. This was her objection to forgiving her offender: "People say that unforgiveness is drinking poison and expecting the other person to get sick—but I have experienced unforgiveness as the only witness to a pain that the rest of the world has moved on from; the one who will sit with me and say, 'Yes, this happened to you. This horrible thing. I remember with you.'"[4]

Take a brief moment right now to honor the pain and trauma that were inflicted on you. What you experienced was real. And in some ways, it is still real. Breathe in and say, "I will honor my pain." Breathe out and say, "I am healing one day at a time."

Sometimes forgiveness seems to be more about letting the offender off the hook, but I believe in certain contexts forgiveness is more about letting the forgiver out of the misery of constantly being triggered and replaying the events.

If you're still replaying the events of your trauma, this tells me three things:

1. Your trauma was profound, the symptoms are still intense, and you're not yet ready to enter the process of forgiveness. That's okay. I will not shame you into forgiving before you are ready to do so.

2. The trauma might still be ongoing.

3. Your pain has not been validated, and the offender hasn't attempted to confess, repent, or repair the relationship, all of which must happen for reconciliation to take place.

The healing process begins when you feel safe and trauma symptoms throughout your body are no longer intense. You can then start processing the intrusive automatic trauma-related thoughts that prevent you from forgiving. The wisdom of Scripture can also help you combat these thoughts and remain in control.

Using God's Wisdom to Soothe Your Thoughts

Let's look at some of those automatic thoughts and see what God's wisdom has to say about them.

An automatic thought says, *Don't forgive, because offenders need to receive their due punishment.*

God says, "The LORD is fighting for you! So be still!" (Exodus 14:14, GW)

An automatic thought says, *You're on your own.*

God says, "I will never leave you nor forsake you." (Joshua 1:5)

An automatic thought says, *If I forgive, others will think of me as weak.*

God says, "My grace is all you need. My power works best in weakness." (2 Corinthians 12:9, NLT)

An automatic thought says, *Who will help me if I don't help myself?*

God says, "God is our refuge and strength, an ever-present help in trouble." (Psalm 46:1)

Write your own message from God to counter what your automatic thoughts are saying:

_____

_____

_____

_____

_____

Going Deep into the Pain Points

Forgiveness is part of God's divine plan to help us heal so that he can use our stories to help others heal. However, the many challenges we encounter along the way can stall the process. This is where we need the wisdom of God to discern how to move forward.

Following are a few especially challenging situations we may face as we seek to forgive those who have harmed us:

- childhood sexual abuse from someone close to us (father, stepfather, mother, uncle, brother, cousin)
- repeated infidelity, lies, or betrayals by a boyfriend or spouse
- the physical abuse of a spouse or partner
- neglect or abandonment
- repeated destructive patterns even after you've forgiven the offender
- prior abuse or mistreatment from someone who is no longer alive

Are you in a challenging situation where you're finding it especially difficult to forgive someone?

As a counselor and pastor, I recommend seeking the support of a mental-health professional to help you discern your next steps in these matters. In the meantime, here are some words of wisdom to keep in mind:

- Forgiveness does not mean remaining in a violent relationship. If someone is continually abusive toward you, whether sexually, physically, or emotionally, and is unwilling to repent, it might be time to consider other options. That person might need more help than you can offer. Get help and take care of yourself and your children, if you have any.

- What people say and what they do should be congruent. If the two don't match and this is a pattern, you're in an unsafe relationship. You can still forgive, but you do not have to remain in the relationship.

- You are *never* the cause of abuse, betrayal, or lying. No one asks for a disingenuous relationship. We're all responsible for controlling our own emotions.

- People who have harmed you don't need to be alive for you to forgive them. Start to free yourself by seeking out a professional therapist to help you work through the trauma they caused.

- Forgiveness doesn't always mean reconciliation. In some cases, it's best to *not* seek reconciliation. But if both of you desire reconciliation, the offender must confess, repent, and commit to living rightly before God and you.

- You can forgive your offender even if they never ask for forgiveness. This is especially important for victims who are not seeking reconciliation.

- Forgiveness doesn't mean not seeking justice. You can forgive and still seek justice for what happened to you, especially if the offender broke the law. Justice and revenge are two different things. Revenge is personal, emotional, and vindictive. Justice is about holding perpetrators accountable for wrongdoing.

Are there any other words of wisdom you would like to add?

Steps to Forgiveness

When you've reached a place in your trauma-healing journey where you feel ready to begin the process of forgiving the person or persons who caused your trauma, it's important to take deliberate steps. Here are some recommendations to help you begin this process:

- Don't rush it. Take things slowly, and make sure you've worked through your trauma symptoms first.

- Take Jesus with you every step of the way.

- Ask God to give you the desire to forgive the person who harmed you. Let go, and God will meet you.

- Ask God to help you take control of automatic thoughts that cause the trauma to replay in your mind. Every time that happens, it's as if you're reliving the trauma. Instead, take every thought captive, and surrender them all in obedience to Jesus Christ (see 2 Corinthians 10:5).

- Don't forgive until you've talked over the situation with Jesus. Accept his help and allow him to bring you comfort through the process of forgiving. Many people forgive verbally before their hearts are ready to stop harboring bitterness and resentment. Give your heart time to heal first.

- Each day, take one small step toward healing and forgiveness.

Affirmations

Positive affirmations are essential not only in your trauma-healing journey but also in the process of forgiving others. The following affirmations can help guide you through the steps of forgiveness and help you take your thoughts captive when you lose focus:

- I love myself more than I hate my offender.

- I will no longer allow my offender's sin toward me to rule my life.

- God has given me control over some things, and I choose to control what will affect me.

- I no longer desire to take unforgiveness, resentment, and bitterness with me everywhere I go.

- I desire to live my life with a greater purpose.

- Releasing my offender from the debt they owe me ultimately sets me free.

- I realize that God's justice is sweeter than my revenge.

- I'm releasing my offender to God. I have no place in my heart for my offender.

- I'm looking forward to a new life that will emerge out of this tragedy.

Dear God, thank you for your grace and mercy. I know I don't deserve your love. But I thank you that by the power of the Holy Spirit through Jesus' sacrifice on the cross and his resurrection you have made me brand new and given me second chances. Father, I pray that you will put the desire in my heart to forgive my offender. As you have forgiven me, I want to forgive so I can live a productive life. I want to live free of any burdens of unforgiveness. Please meet me as I start taking steps toward forgiveness. Amen.

QUESTIONS TO EXPLORE

1. Have you accepted forgiveness from God through Jesus Christ?

2. What is your journey of forgiveness? Have you ever had to forgive someone for an offense they committed against you? What was your process?

3. Do you currently have someone in your heart that you would like to forgive?

4. What has been holding you back from forgiving?

5. What do you need to help you take a step toward forgiving this person?

FROM HEAD TO BODY

Pain and fear of being injured again are often at the center of unforgiveness. When we become dysregulated, we cannot be present long enough to manage the discomfort of painful feelings. Repetition exercises can help us develop ways of safely holding difficult feelings and trauma responses so that we can stay regulated thorough stress and discomfort.[5]

With these words in mind, let's do a repetition exercise that will help you move some of the pain held in your body.

Repetition Exercise

This body activity is borrowed from Thema Bryant-Davis:

Imagine that your body is water. Begin to move your head and neck as though they flow easily like water. Now move your shoulders, arms, and hands as if they are waves of water. Next move your rib cage and chest in a smooth circle. Begin to move your hips in easy waterlike movements. Let your legs now move with smooth motions carrying your body around the room in waves of peace. Now sit down and let your feet move around in front of you like cascading waves of water. Finally hug yourself and say, "I care about myself. I value myself. I deserve care." Breathe in and out slowly seven times.[u]

Reflection from Nature

Read and try to remember this affirmation: *I trust that there is good in me and good in the world.*

List Activity

The sun can warm, and the sun can also burn. Likewise, people have the capacity to do good or do harm. Write the names below of those who have warmed/nurtured you and then the names of those who have burned/harmed you. Some people may have done both. If so, put them on both lists. What feelings come up when you review your lists?

Once you've finished these activities, spend some time processing the experience in your journal or with a friend. Remember, trauma healing doesn't happen overnight. Keep these practices and others I've recommended in your toolbox to use over time as you grow more resilient.

14

FORGIVING YOURSELF

If we confess our sins, he is faithful and just and
will forgive us our sins and purify us from all unrighteousness.

1 JOHN 1:9

Unhealed trauma often leads to more trauma. Living your life in trauma and unforgiveness can lead to bitterness and resentment that perpetuate cycles of pain. At some point, your unhealed parts will cause you to make decisions from a place of pain that will spill over onto someone else, harming both you and others in your life. You will need to go through the process of forgiveness, not only seeking the forgiveness of others but also learning to forgive yourself. As a therapist, I've observed that one of the hardest things for many to do in the trauma-healing journey is to forgive themselves for past mistakes and failures. Sometimes it seems easier to forgive others and be gracious toward them than toward ourselves.

While volunteering in the Dallas jail years ago, I met many women who made life decisions that resulted in grave consequences. Some lost their employment. Many lost contact with their families. Others lost the love of their lives through countless instances of betrayal. The decision many of these women grieved the most was the one that led to losing custody of their children. It's important to note that most of the women I met in jail had an extensive history of unhealed trauma. They'd come into our sessions with shame and debilitating guilt. The thought of moving forward would often overwhelm them. Their failures loomed so large that they couldn't fathom working through the process of living rightly. They'd even convince themselves that healing was too hard. It seemed easier to not attempt making amends with their families or getting on the right path. So they would remain stuck, unable to break destructive patterns or take steps to forgive themselves.

Living abundant lives as followers of Christ is sometimes reduced to good or bad behavior. Many churches seem to focus a great deal of attention on behavior modification so we'll look the part and ensure good standing with others and with God. But if our behavior is deemed bad, there's no real process for accountability or restoration with God and others.

Before we can move toward forgiving and loving ourselves, we must address the elephant in the room that we often try to avoid: sin. We don't always do a good job handling sin, since it's often interpreted simply as "bad behavior." In a sermon about sin, one of my dear pastor friends, José Humphreys, said this: "If you think sin is just bad behavior, you have a thin view of sin, and if you have a thin view of sin, you have a thin view of grace."[1]

If sin is categorized only as bad behavior, people feel worse about getting caught for breaking the rules than causing actual pain. Pastor José defines *sin* as "the breakdown of relationships with

God and others." In the sermon, he used a quote from Gustavo Gutiérrez that says, "Sin is a breach of friendship with God and others. . . . According to the Bible, [sin is] the ultimate cause of poverty, injustice, and the oppression in which persons live."[2]

Let's pause for a second and let these words penetrate. Sin is not just about bad behavior; it's about the rupture, the breakdown, the disruption, and the disturbance it causes in our relationships with God and others. Imagine if we were to care more about that breakdown than the actual behavior.

In my line of work, I often see the corroding impact of sin not just on individuals but on generations as well. At some point in a client's lineage, for example, a disturbance (sin) tore apart the relationship between family members. This disturbance was so traumatic that it rendered members of the family incapable of healing or justice. There was no accountability, no repentance, no reparations, and no forgiveness. The opportunity for a right relationship with God and others came and went. The sin festered and was passed on to the next generation to handle without any context. Eventually it worked its way down to the next generation and the next.

When sin becomes a generational issue, before we know it we see women, like the ones I met in jail, who are struggling with deep-seated issues but are unable to pinpoint how and when it all started. This is what Gutiérrez means when he says that sin is "the ultimate cause of poverty, injustice, and the oppression in which persons live." Without healing and forgiveness, this pervasive process will persist.

The question is *How do we even begin to address sin in our lives?* How can we start addressing not just sinful behaviors but also their deeply destructive impact on our relationships? The first step is creating awareness of how sin has impacted our current relationships.

Sin and Your Relationships

God created us for relationships. But where there is deeply rooted sin, a few things will happen in our relationships with others. The first is a tendency to isolate ourselves. I'm not just referring to romantic relationships; I'm referring to all kinds of relationships where we can be seen. When there's sin in our lives, the tendency to hide is strong. Instead of seeking out relationships with mutual accountability, we find ways to bypass them. In some relationships, we may blame others for not being good friends. Or we may put little to no effort into cultivating a relationship and eventually stop showing up altogether.

A second tendency to be aware of when there is deeply rooted sin in our lives is cycling through relationships. We may lack the ability to develop or maintain good friendships. If there is no longevity in our friendships, we may cut people off left and right and start over with new friends.

Lastly, when sin is deeply rooted in our lives, we tend to have little tolerance for working through conflicts in our relationships. Whenever there's a hint of conflict, we may find ways to evade the responsibility and not do the work necessary to resolve it.

Of course, these tendencies can be the result of trauma, so we need to be aware of that. But sometimes the trauma we experience can result in sinning against others. That is why the healing journey is vital for thriving relationships with ourselves, God, and others.

A number of the people I see in counseling show up because whatever is going on in their lives is impacting their relationships. Your engagement in relationships can help you become aware of sin in your life. It takes great humility to submit to accountability, allowing others to see you and speak into your life for your benefit. Awareness is key when you need to confront sin. And relationships are vital in supporting that process.

Confession and Apology

Once you become aware of sin and accept responsibility for it, the next step is to humbly confess it. There's something beautiful and restorative about confessing how you have caused harm in a relationship.

As Gustavo Gutiérrez says, "Sin is a breach of friendship with God and others," so to repair the breach, we need to confess our sin to God and others. God is merciful and full of compassion, and we can be confident that when we confess our sins and repent, he will be true to his promise to "forgive us our sins and purify us from all unrighteousness" (1 John 1:9).

The process of confession can be both communal and individual. I've found communal confession to be an uplifting exercise that brings great spiritual release. Individual confession can include any number of postures, such as spending time in prayer, writing in your journal, or communing with the Spirit in silence and solitude.

At times, it may be difficult to find adequate words to express to God the ways you have broken your relationship with him and how you feel about what has happened. I've found the following prayer helpful when words fail me. Every time I read this prayer, it slows me down, and tears sometimes well up as I'm reminded of my sin. To personalize these words from the Book of Common Prayer, I've reframed this communal prayer in the first person:

> *Most merciful God, I confess that I have sinned against you in thought, word, and deed, by what I have done, and by what I have left undone. I have not loved you with my whole heart; I have not loved my neighbors as myself. I am truly sorry and I humbly repent. For the sake of your Son Jesus Christ, have mercy on me and forgive me; that I may delight in your will, and walk in your ways, to the glory of your name. Amen.*[3]

Whether you pray this prayer or confess your sins to God in your own words, you can trust that you have received his forgiveness and are free to step into the path of righteous living with God and your neighbors. You are also free to reach out daily for the grace of the Holy Spirit to stay on that path of right living before God and others.

I've worked with clients who have committed one of the most traumatic breaches in a relationship: betrayal. Sometimes confession seems painful to both parties, and I remind them that it can be a connecting activity. They often give me a blank look before I share this explanation: If sin is a breach of friendship, imagine what telling the truth through confession can do for a relationship. I believe that when there's true confession and true repentance, some relationships can be restored in time.

The following tips from Harriet Lerner are helpful for approaching confession and repentance. An apology is often a great step forward, but, as Lerner puts it, a true apology

1. does not include the word *but*,

2. keeps the focus on your actions and not on the other person's response,

3. includes an offer of reparation or restitution that fits the situation,

4. does not overdo it with one's own pain and remorse,

5. doesn't get caught up in who's more to blame or who started it,

6. requires that you do your best to avoid a repeat performance,

7. should not serve to silence or be used to avoid a difficult talk,

8. should not risk making the hurt party feel worse in order to make the apologizer feel better,

9. does not ask the hurt party to do anything, and

10. recognizes when "I'm sorry" is not enough and work is required to restore trust.[4]

The reality is that even when there's true confession, true repentance, and a true apology, reconciliation isn't guaranteed. Some hurts in a relationship run too deep to repair, even when forgiveness has taken place. If you're seeking reconciliation in a relationship, be present and patient with the process. As the offended party works through their own pain, they'll need time for healing and recovery work. They will also need time and space to discern whether the relationship can be reconciled.

You Are Worthy of Love

Now for the most difficult part: accepting God's forgiveness and forgiving yourself. When I've taken all the steps I'm aware of to deal with my sin, I often sing this line of Donnie McClurkin's song "Stand": "After you've done all you can, you just stand."[5] That's the only thing left to do when you've done all you can.

In this chapter, I've mentioned several ways to address sin in our lives. After you've become aware of the pain you've caused; after you've confessed and repented of your sin and offered a true apology; after you've made amends and offered restitution, the only thing left to do is stand.

Stand and let God restore you. I believe the process of restoration isn't instantaneous in the human body. The body needs time to catch up to the grace of God. It takes time to learn to live as a restored and forgiven child of God. It takes time to accept that

God sees you as precious and worthy. Take it in one day at a time, and breathe in the goodness of God. Walk in the light of each new day to dispel any feelings of shame. Stand in the truth that you've reconciled with God and done the work to reconcile with those you have caused pain.

The very last part of this equation is relieving yourself of any debt you internally believe you still owe. Many times, you might find shame lingering, telling you that you're not good enough, not worthy of forgiveness. In those moments, it's important to do two things: (1) look at God and the reconciliation work you've done with him and (2) turn to the work you've already put in to ensure you have truly repented and have done your part to make amends.

The truth is, you are loved and worthy of love. Even on your worst day, the banner over you is love. Through love and forgiveness, you can redefine yourself from this marker in your story. God still has great work to accomplish through you. Will you allow love to lead you into the greatest version of yourself? You are capable of receiving love and giving love. You are not ruined for good works. There is goodness in you. There is love in you. There is purpose in you. Allow love for God, yourself, and others to lead you.

QUESTIONS TO EXPLORE

1. When it comes to forgiving yourself for mistakes and failures in your life, how do you confront them?

2. What is your process of confessing your sin to God? To others?

3. How do you feel after you have confessed, repented, and committed to living rightly before God?

4. How do you build confidence when your life has been shattered?

FROM HEAD TO BODY

Forgiving yourself can conjure up feelings of shame and unworthiness. Shame can often show up in your body—shoulders slumped, head down, posture slouched. This next exercise will help you lift up your head, accept God's forgiveness, and build your confidence.

To begin, plant your feet firmly on the ground beneath you. Then lift your chest and head. Extend both of your arms in a wide-open posture, with palms and face lifted toward the sun. Take a breath and hold it for about sixty seconds. Repeat this a few times, holding your breath as long as your body needs it. Pay attention to how your body feels before and after the pose. It can make you feel energized and empowered.

REDISCOVERING HOPE

*Early the next morning Abraham took some food and a
skin of water and gave them to Hagar. He set them on her
shoulders and then sent her off with the boy. She went
on her way and wandered in the Desert of Beersheba.
When the water in the skin was gone, she put the boy
under one of the bushes. Then she went off and sat down
about a bowshot away, for she thought, "I cannot watch
the boy die." And as she sat there, she began to sob.
God heard the boy crying, and the angel of God
called to Hagar from heaven and said to her, "What is
the matter, Hagar? Do not be afraid; God has heard the
boy crying as he lies there. Lift the boy up and take him
by the hand, for I will make him into a great nation."
Then God opened her eyes and she saw a well of water. So she
went and filled the skin with water and gave the boy a drink.*

GENESIS 21:14-19

I once read that some people have "the privilege of hopelessness"
in life.[1] That phrase stopped me dead in my tracks and led to days
of pondering. It had never occurred to me that for some people,
hopelessness is a privilege. That phrase felt familiar, like something
I'd experienced before. And I had. Every trip I've taken to Haiti,
Kenya, and the DRC, as well as the times I've spent in certain communities in the United States, I've seen firsthand how hopelessness is a privilege. Communities that have spent many years and
decades living under oppression and prolonged trauma know that

if their hope to survive were to disappear, they'd lose everything. When all resources are gone and sources of comfort are hard to find, there's one thing we must not lose sight of or death would win—and that is hope. A woman like Hagar had no choice but to hope one more time; otherwise, it would have meant a sort of despair that could have led to her demise and the death of her son.

Holding On to Hope

All around the world, I see women holding on to hope because they want to live for what could be. That is the definition of *hope*: allowing the possibilities of what our lives could be to give us the strength to keep moving forward just one more day. In this chapter, I want the women who don't have the privilege of hopelessness to teach us about hope.

Just to be clear, I'm not talking about just any kind of hope. I've known people who place their hope in the government and politicians to show mercy and justice, hope in people to behave morally, hope in the family to treat them as they deserve, or even hope in other Christians to behave like Christ with love, fairness, and compassion. Hope in people and things will surely leave us disillusioned at some point. What I'm talking about is the hope found through the life, death, and resurrection of Jesus Christ. That's the only hope I pray we continue to lean into, especially when we're faced with the pain of this world.

Even though we live with the tension that some prayers will go unanswered, and some prayers for deliverance and physical healing might not be met with a miracle, we ask God to deliver us and heal us anyway. Right now, injustice, trauma, pain, and suffering are still present realities. But we hold on and seek justice anyway. We do this because all throughout the Bible, we see a "great cloud of witnesses" (Hebrews 12:1) who can testify that God is real, he performs miracles, he loves us, he died and was resurrected, and he desires for us to flourish. We read about a cloud of witnesses who can testify, "I have now seen the One who sees me" (Genesis 16:13). Ancestors have gone before us as witnesses who not only survived but also left us with a legacy of faith to stand on. We, too, stand as witnesses through the gift of the Holy Spirit. The Spirit of God in us has not only allowed us to see and experience the greatness of God, but he has sustained us and transformed us through many dark seasons.

Because of these witnesses, we believe that Christ will return once again to bring forth a new heaven and a new earth. In Revelation 21, the apostle John wrote,

> I saw "a new heaven and a new earth," for the first heaven and the first earth had passed away. . . . "God's dwelling place is now among the people, and he will dwell with them. They will be his people, and God himself will be with them and be their God. 'He will wipe every tear from their eyes. There will be no more death' or mourning or crying or pain, for the old order of things has passed away."
>
> He who was seated on the throne said, "I am making everything new!"
>
> REVELATION 21:1, 3-5

Because of these witnesses in the Bible, we can hold on to the hope that God will make everything new. He will create a new heaven and a new earth that will be free from trauma, pain, suffering, and injustice. In this new heaven and earth, peace and joy will reign. And "his kingdom will never end" (Luke 1:33). This is our source of hope.

In Genesis 21, Hagar reappeared, and her story was recentered. This time she wasn't running away for her safety. She and her son were sent away, kicked out to die in the desert. In fact, they came close to death, but the Lord intervened once again. The Lord preserved Hagar's life and the life of her son, Ishmael.

There's a line from Alice Walker's book *The Color Purple* that encapsulates Hagar's life narrative: "All my life I had to fight."[2] All of Hagar's days were spent fighting for her life and the life of her son. From what we can tell from the text, Hagar never stopped fighting, and she was never delivered out of the desert. So how is it that she continued to have the strength to survive? Again: Hopelessness is a privilege. Hagar did not have the privilege of being hopeless. Hopelessness would have been the end of her life and the life of her son. She had to fight to survive, and part of her survival was to not give up on hope.

Remaining Hopeful in Difficult Times

Let's be honest, though, remaining hopeful day in and day out when God is silent has got to be the hardest exercise of faith. All the women I've worked with around the world would agree. However, there's a Haitian saying that people use whenever they're faced with the choice of walking away or remaining faithful and hopeful: "Nou pa gen chwa," which in English is translated, "We don't have any other choice." That saying captures hope when it's hard. We don't have any other choice but to remain hopeful, because where else do we go and whom else can we turn to? As the psalmist said in Psalm 73, "Whom have I in heaven but [God]?" (verse 25).

When hope is met with disillusionment, people all over the world join together to lament and worship as a discipline. They come together to sing and pray for encouragement. And their lament gives way to hope in Christ Jesus.

In the Haitian culture, this is a common hymn of comfort in difficult times:

Sere m pi pre ou, tou pre kè ou
Ou se trezò mwen, ou se Sovè m tou
Kenbe m, o kenbe m, Bondye damou
Fè m jwenn yon kote pou m kache nan ou

Draw me closer to you, right by your heart
You are my treasure and my Savior, too
Hold me, O hold me, God of love
Find me a place to hide in you

This is the cry of women who don't have the privilege of hopelessness. *Hold me, God. Hide me, God. Find a place for me to hide when the world around me is unsafe.*

Then they sing some more . . .

Jezu se tout bagay pou mwen
Lapè, lajwa, lavi
Se li ki fòs mwen tou lè jou
Mwen ta tonbe san li
Lè-m santi-m tris, se li-m chache
Si-l pa te la, sa mwen ta fè
Lè-m santi-m tris, li fè mwen ge
Li renmen-m

Jesus is all the world to me
My peace, my joy, my life
He is my strength for all the days
Without him I would have fallen
When I'm sad, it's him I seek
If he wasn't here, what would I do?
When I'm sad, he makes me glad
He loves me

This is the anthem of hope for women who don't have the privilege of hopelessness. *God, I have hope in nothing else; you're all I have.* This is the lament of women who have nothing tangible to hold on to but the treasure they have found in Christ Jesus. So they sing to express their desperation. And at times, the songs of lament turn to moans of lament.

Let's not forget Negro spirituals, songs of lament and comfort that oppressed African Americans would sing. These songs reverberate like the hymns of the Haitian people. These spirituals were a source of strength and hope for the oppressed and persecuted to help them survive and hold on for just one more day. Listen to these words of hope:

> *I say I'm gonna hold out,*
> *Hold out, hold out.*
> *I say that I'm gonna hold out,*
> *Until my change comes.*
>
> *I promised the Lord that I would hold out,*
> *Hold out, hold out.*
> *I promised the Lord that I would hold out,*
> *Wait until my change comes.*[3]

Can you hear the people sing? Can you hear them cry out to God for strength to survive until change comes? The Lord was their source of resilience and hope to survive so that the next generation could have a chance at life.

The Shadow of Hope

My first journey to the continent of Africa was to Kenya. There I encountered a type of worship that was reminiscent of my people in Haiti. Sounding like angels, the women sang melodious songs of worship in Swahili: "Ni wewe bwana, ni wewe, ni wewe bwana, ni wewe" ("It is you, Lord"). They cried out to God through song. They danced and clapped their hands. The energy in the room filled the atmosphere. Every last one of us seemed filled with the Spirit of God, encouraged and strengthened to go on for one more day. There's something about these songs of lament, these songs of worship, that uplifts us and sets us on a path toward hope.

As trauma occurs in our lives, we will wade through the sea of hope and hopelessness. I pray we may continue to glean hope from Hagar and other women from all around the world who do not have the privilege of hopelessness. Even if it's only a shadow of hope.

Austin Channing Brown has said, "This is the shadow of hope. Knowing that we may never see the realization of our dreams, and yet still showing up."[4]

Our God of hope, we call on your name today to help us hold on to hope. I call on your name today, especially for the sister reading this right now who has nothing else to hope for. I pray she can find her hope in you. I pray, Holy Spirit, that the strength and tenacity of women from all over the world may be reminders to go on for just one more day. Amen.

QUESTIONS TO EXPLORE

1. When you hear the phrase *the privilege of hopelessness,* what resonates with you?

2. Has there ever been a season when you've felt hopeless? If so, share what caused your feelings of hopelessness.

3. What's your strategy for moving out of hopelessness?

4. What's been helpful for you when you feel hopeless?

FROM HEAD TO BODY

Moving from hopelessness to hopefulness takes patience and intentionality. An exercise that encourages hopefulness is the traditional upward-facing-dog yoga pose. This is a great body practice because, at the end, it leaves your chest wide open, looking forward to the future and new possibilities.

To begin, grab a yoga mat, a towel, or a sheet. Lie on your stomach, place your hands flat on the ground underneath your shoulders, and push your torso off the ground while pressing your tailbone and the tops of your feet down. Press your chest forward and look straight ahead. This practice helps open your chest, which makes taking deep breaths easier. Take a deep breath, hold it for twenty to thirty seconds, and then breathe out. Pay attention to your breath and how your body is feeling.

After releasing your breath, move back into the beginning pose. Repeat the exercise a few times.

EMBRACING JOY

*This day I call the heavens and the earth as
witnesses against you that I have set before you
life and death, blessings and curses. Now choose
life, so that you and your children may live.*

DEUTERONOMY 30:19

*May the God of hope fill you with all joy and peace
as you trust in him, so that you may overflow
with hope by the power of the Holy Spirit.*

ROMANS 15:13

One day I was scrolling through Facebook aimlessly, as I often do when I'm bored or trying to evade something difficult. As I scrolled past a video, something struck me that warranted a closer look. The video was of a group of women from Haiti doing laundry. They sat on large stones along the river. The water was just inches away, flowing over their feet. The river provided easy access for washing clothes. The women had bars of soap and buckets in front of them filled with clothes in soapy water.

As they picked up each item of clothing, scrubbing and wringing out the dirt, they broke into a worship song:

O Letènèl, mwen konte sou ou,
Ou menm sèl, lè W pale, pèsòn pa ka opoze
O, bon Papa mwen fikse je m sou ou
Mwen konnen ou p ap abandone m

Pale pou mwen, senyè pale pou mwen
Aji pou mwen, senyè aji pou mwen
Kanpe pou mwen, senyè kanpe pou mwen
O, o ou se tout sa m genyen

Oh Eternal God, I'm counting on you,
You alone; when you speak, no one can oppose
Oh good Father, I'm fixing my eyes on you
I know you will not abandon me

Speak for me, God, speak for me
Move on my behalf, God, move on my behalf
Stand for me, God, stand for me
Oh, oh, you are everything I have

One lady led, and the others joined her in this beautiful, melodic hymn. Everyone knew their part. Added to this ensemble were the angelic voices of pubescent children who were helping with the laundry. As they sang, I could see some of the other children swimming and playing on the opposite side of the river. The sounds of children laughing, water splashing, and women singing blended together to create a symphony of joy. I was struck by their joy. It caused me to pause, to take notice, to learn, and to breathe it in.

It instantly catapulted me into memories of my childhood in Haiti. It reminded me of the feeling I get every time I visit my sisters on the mission field on the African continent and in Haiti. It reminded me of moments of laughter, dance, and singing in the midst of some of life's most traumatic seasons. That feeling is joy.

Resisting Despair

Theologian Willie James Jennings once shared in an interview that "joy [is] an act of resistance against despair and its forces."[1] Ever since I watched that interview, I haven't been able to reject the thought of joy in the midst of pain. I've been on a quest to make sense of these seemingly opposing concepts.

We have walked through a book filled with real stories of trauma—stories that have caused soul and spirit death. If any of the trauma victims decided to live the rest of their days in despair, most people would understand. However, Jennings drew attention to yet another vital component of surviving trauma: joy. His advice for resisting despair is through joy. Joy is the defiant act of resistance against the despair that is often present in trauma.

Which begs the question: Why must we resist despair? Why should we wrestle against it? Why should we fight to survive and live through trauma? The pain of trauma is so invasive and consuming, why can't we just allow the despair of trauma to have the final word? We'd all understand if one chose the path of despair birthed from trauma.

For many who have gone through trauma, death is an imminent threat that looms daily. It wants to win. Its job is to claim another victim. Its job is to annihilate and destroy you, along with your present and future. I have witnessed many who are living in the flesh but are dead in the spirit. There's nothing more painful than living physically while being dead emotionally and spiritually.

Deuteronomy 30:19 makes a compelling proposition: "This day I call the heavens and the earth as witnesses against you that I have set before you life and death, blessings and curses. Now choose life, so that you and your children may live." This verse has been an anchor for me through many seasons when despair wanted to claim my life. Jennings says we must resist "despair and all the ways [it] wants to drive us toward death, and wants to make death the final word. And death in this regard is not simply the end of life, but it's death in all its signatures . . . all the ways in which life can be strangled."[2]

The verse in Deuteronomy makes a convincing case to resist despair while choosing life. It says, "Here's why you must resist: 'so that you and your children may live.'" The first reason to choose life is so that we may personally live. Meaning that if we choose life, we'll see the gift that it is. We will have learned vital lessons about the journey that makes living worth it. Every day we choose life, we get to be part of God's mission to tear down systems that don't allow the flourishing of all God's children and create systems that do. We get to step into our greatest calling. We get to join God in his work on earth. Every day we get to reflect the beauty and glory of God. So choose life! Even if in the moment you can't see the point of living, just choose life and keep choosing life. In doing so, you will find the meaning and purpose for your life.

The second reason to choose life is so that our children will live. In other words, if we choose life, we will produce living legacies. In the case of Hagar, if she had not chosen life, not only would she have died, but her son would have died as well. Hagar's choice to live resulted in the fulfillment of the promise God made to her in the desert: "I will increase your descendants so much that they will be too numerous to count" (Genesis 16:10). And that he did.

As Wilda Gafney says, "Ultimately Hagar escapes her slave-holders and abusers and receives her inheritance from God, and God fulfills all of God's promises to her."[3] Yes! Hagar did not die in the wilderness. She fought to hold on, and with the provision of God, she became what God had promised.

Joy in the Midst of Pain

Women all over the world wake up every day choosing life because of their children. They want their children to live. They want their children to have opportunities they did not receive. They want their children to have the lives they didn't have. Even if you don't have children, choosing your own life allows others to live as well. I love this insightful idea: "As we let our own light shine, we unconsciously give other people permission to do the same."[4] Healing is released when we hear a person's story of survival. It's as if something in our souls rises up and says, "If she can heal and find new life, so can I." Choosing your life inspires others to choose their own lives. Life is worth living because only then can we be witnesses to our own strength, courage, and redemption stories.

I'm grateful to have been a witness to all the women in my family who went before me, who fought and won their battles against despair. They chose joy instead of giving in to death and despair. Joy is their legacy to me. I'm here because they chose to resist despair through joy. Joy is the path toward choosing life. Joy is the path to resisting despair.

In the previous chapter, I talked about hope. Hope that Christ will return and bring about peace. The hope of the risen Savior is both now and not yet. Hope is optimism that things will change in the future. It's having the faith to hold on. Hope says, "Even if I don't see things change in my lifetime, perhaps my children or the next generation will." Fighting against despair and death in the present must be swaddled in future hope. That future hope makes living joyfully in the present possible, even when the present looks grim. Joy helps us survive the now as we wait and hope for the not yet in the future.

Joy in the midst of pain and suffering is not only possible but vital to survival.

I remember after my brother died in the middle of the Christmas holiday, every last one of us wanted to cancel our family gathering. We were in shock and pain. After some conversations, we decided to push through our grief and gather together. My mother assumed her usual post in the kitchen. She was in deep pain from losing her only son, but she pushed through and cooked a Christmas dinner of rice and beans, griot (pork), chicken in Kreyol sauce, and plantains that my brother requested days before. Every Christmas, my brother and his wife were responsible for the bingo games and all the prizes everyone in the family often fought for. But this Christmas, days after her husband died, my sister-in-law pushed through without him, and everyone fought over the prizes as usual. My five sisters and I sat around the table as we often did and held conversations. At times with tears in our eyes, but grateful to be around each other.

Fifteen nieces and nephews pushed through their grief and hosted game night as they had planned, with lots of shouting and impromptu dancing. They came up with the idea of singing Kirk Franklin's "Till We Meet Again" at the funeral, which was set for a few days after Christmas. The morning after game night, they all gathered around the dining-room table to practice the harmony. Each time they messed up, there'd be a huge wave of laughter and joy that soared throughout the house. If the neighbors were listening closely, they never would have known we were facing one of the greatest losses in our family.

I can't fully explain it because I don't understand how we were able to find joy in the midst of such devastation. I don't understand how joy can coexist with pain. I often think that the joy we experienced during those times together is what helped us push through the funeral and the days ahead. People on the outside might judge the joy we expressed in those times as inauthentic, but our joy was real and necessary for survival. We can't apologize or feel shame for expressing joy that propels us onward.

Jennings says that two things are needed for joy to be cultivated in our lives: (1) "people who have learned how to ride the winds of chaos" with joy and can show us the way, and (2) "a willingness . . . to hold on to Life, even when there is very little that makes sense."[5] We've seen how expressing joy as a community can heal. In the community, we see examples of previous generations surviving through joy. I learned survival through joy from my mother, who would wake up very early every Sunday morning and begin preparing breakfast and dinner. As she did, she would sing. I would sometimes hear her sing and weep in the same breath. Throughout her life, I've never seen her give in to despair. Her songs of joy helped her push through the pain to survive. Her example taught me about leaning on joy to help me push through days of despair. Community not only helps us lament; it also teaches us about joy. We need community to lead us into joy.

The second thing we need for cultivating joy is the willingness to survive by finding joy in the midst of our pain. There's truth in what Alice Walker says: "Don't wait around for other people to be happy for you. Any happiness you get you've got to make yourself."[6] There's a part of the healing process that is completely up to you. To step into joy, we must first *want* to live with joy. That willingness will create opportunities for us to experience joy.

Joy is possible. It is all around us. If you are willing, you can take part in it. If you look closely in society, especially among oppressed people groups, you will see it. I see it in little hut churches in Haiti with wooden benches and dusty floors, where well-dressed women and men show up with joy, grateful for the gift of life and a brand-new day. With their hands lifted up and mouths filled with praise, they clap, sing, and dance, creating a ripple of joy that carries them through the challenges of the coming week.

I often see it in New York City, where crowds gather around dancers in the street.

I see it when African dancers throw their bodies into different moves, sending off the electrifying energy of joy.

I see it when African worshipers ululate—expressing their joy through high-pitched shouts of praise.

I see it when children in the city run through the bursting waters of an open hydrant on a hot summer day.

I see it in hip-hop dancers who create new moves that leave you speechless.

I feel it as I watch opera singers expressing emotions and drama through vocal runs, trills, and leaps.

I see it when Haitians drop that Kompa beat at weddings and graduations.

I feel it when I'm outside on a nature walk immersed in God's creation.

I see it and feel it in Black women daring to be fully seen in how they dress, walk, talk, and take up space.

Joy is all around us, ready to be experienced even in the midst of struggle. Joy is ready to help shift our energy from despair to resistance. Joy is available to aid us in our fight for survival. Joy is possible if you are willing.

Our God of joy, we thank you for being the source of our joy. We thank you that even when our worlds have turned upside down, joy is not too far away. I thank you for your Spirit, who does not allow joy to be based solely on our circumstances or relegated to those who are rich with access to experiencing a life of luxury. I rejoice that joy is for me and for my sister reading this prayer, wherever she may be. I pray for your Spirit to daily lead us toward opportunities where we can experience joy. In the name of the Father, the Son, and the Holy Spirit, amen.

QUESTIONS TO EXPLORE

1. Deuteronomy 30:19 challenges us to "choose life." In what ways are you choosing life?

2. What prevents you from choosing life and experiencing joy?

3. What do you think about joy as a form of resistance?

4. When was the last time you expressed joy? Please share the experience.

5. Have you seen joy expressed around you? Share a few of your experiences with joy.

FROM HEAD TO BODY

Psalm 30:11 says, "You turned my wailing into dancing; you removed my sackcloth and clothed me with joy."

It is fitting to end this book with a recommendation to dance. Find a place where you feel free to dance—in your home, at a party, at a dance class, or some other venue. Grab your children, grab your girlfriends, call the neighbors, have a block party, and just dance. Turn on the boom box and dance to the music or make your own. Just dance. Allow yourself to experience joy. Allow yourself to laugh and play. Give yourself permission to break up the pain and just dance. You are worthy of joy. Create some space to dance before the Lord, "for he is good," and "his love endures forever" (Psalm 136:1).

EPILOGUE

When it came time to give this book an official title, my editor and
I brainstormed several possibilities, none of which felt quite right.
It was very important for me to come up with a title that resonated
with women readers who have suffered from all kinds of trauma
and pain. So I took a few days to join forces with Hagar and with
the women I've met around the world. I posed the following question to my friends and my community: "In the depth of your pain,
what have you often wondered?" The question that resonated the
most for all of us was *Does God see me?* Immediately I knew this
had to be the title of my book. My editor agreed!

Truth be told, over the past decade, I've asked this question
more than I care to admit. Even while writing this book, I encountered many challenges that made me wonder, *Does God see me?*

Now I know it's not a question I utter in isolation. It's a universal question. It is in the hearts of all who have dealt with some kind of trauma, pain, and suffering.

Hagar wrestled with this question too! And when God answered, she proclaimed in shock, excitement, and amazement, "You are the God who sees me" (Genesis 16:13).

My encouragement to each of you is to not shy away from this question. Ask it as many times as you need to. Let your pain be known, and let it be heard. My hope is that you will be met in the wilderness like Hagar to proclaim that God sees you. Every time I ask the question, a part of me waits in anticipation for God to show me that he sees me. May you also ask in anticipation for God to show you that he sees you.

I pray to one day meet Hagar, the woman whose life told so many of our stories. Hagar did not die in the wilderness without hope. Wilda Gafney says, "There is hope. Sarai will not destroy her; Hagar will survive. In [Genesis] 16:10, Hagar receives the first divine annunciation to a woman in the canon of a promised child and promise of a dynasty. Hagar will become the Mother of Many Peoples."[1]

Hagar is a mother to all of us. The woman who taught us to fight, to hold on, and to dare to hope for a better tomorrow. Hagar taught us about resilience and perseverance. She revealed to us God's posture of great intimacy toward the oppressed. She taught us how to have a truthful and vulnerable relationship with God even in the depth of our pain. She occupied a special place with God. She named God and lived to tell about it.

Hagar gave me back a sense of hope, and that hope has translated into writing this book. When I see her, I will thank her because she has made me feel seen and less alone in my struggles. She became a friend who helped me live to tell my story. And she has helped me over and over to find the answer to the question

"Does God see me?" Yes, yes! God sees me, and I have seen the One who sees me.

My friends, hear these words of benediction as you go:

The LORD bless you
 and keep you;
the LORD make his face shine on you
 and be gracious to you;
the LORD turn his face toward you
 and give you peace.

NUMBERS 6:24-26

May the God of hope fill you with all joy and peace as you trust in him, so that you may overflow with hope by the power of the Holy Spirit.

ROMANS 15:13

Acknowledgments

To my one and only little bro, Sonny—thank you. Thank you for blessing me with the gift of your friendship, though our stories did not intersect at birth like the stories of many other siblings because of our parents' painful migration. When we met, we instantly knew our assignment as siblings. We became loyal allies. Being siblings meant forming a bond that could never be broken, no matter how far apart we were or how angry we were at each other, not even by death. Your presence in my life in those early years in the US made life bearable and meaningful. You became my laughing buddy. The way we would laugh hysterically over the silliest things was life-giving. I often wondered what it was like having all sisters (five, to be exact). I learned at your funeral how proud you were of us, describing us each by personality and vocation. It warmed my heart when someone at your funeral said, "So you're the sister who's a pastor living in Texas? He talked about his sisters all the time." Though I continue to mourn not having had enough time to live near each other as adults to enjoy our friendship, I believe you've given me enough to carry me through the rest of my journey. This book would not be possible if not for you. Your passing gave me the boldness and sense of urgency to write from a place of authenticity to help people heal from trauma and meet God in their healing journey. Thank you for constantly whispering in my ear, *Go, sis! You got this*. I miss you every day. Till we meet again.

To my dad, Jacques—thank you. Thank you for fighting so I and my siblings could have a chance at living to our full potential. You risked everything to leave Haiti and made a way for not only us but countless others. Your belief that everyone should have a chance at flourishing continues to be the energy behind my work. I often mourn not having had enough time or healing on this side of heaven to experience a healthy father/daughter relationship, but I rejoice in the countless ways you've blessed me and set me on a path toward my destiny.

To my grandmother, Ti Anne—thank you. Thank you for loving me well. Thank you for being the first person to teach me what love felt like.

To Christopher Morand and Gyto Blain—I mention your names as a testimony of your life here on earth. Losing you both in 2019, back-to-back, will forever mark us. You are loved and missed.

To my husband—thank you. Thank you for always believing in me in word and deed. You have been constant in creating space for me to be who God has called me to be and do what God has called me to do.

To my sons—thank you. Thank you for being vessels for me to pour all my love on. You made it safe for me to love you without the fear of rejection. Thank you for your confidence in me. I'm grateful for all the ways you build me up.

To my sisters and nieces—thank you. Thank you for listening, for being present, for showing up, for laughing with me and offering me the occasional meal. Thank you for being a sounding board, for letting me process ideas of this book with you. You are all the wind beneath my wings.

To my mom—thank you. Thank you for the gift of life. Thank you for teaching me about perseverance and resilience by how you've lived through trial and tribulation. You've taught me how to hold on when life becomes unsteady.

To the rest of my family—thank you. Your collective energy, especially in the past few years, has given me life, and that life has given me the confidence to step into my calling.

Nothing significant we do in life is accomplished alone. God used a whole tribe of people to bring this project to fruition.

To my friend Julie Lyons—thank you. Thank you for allowing God to use you on this book-writing journey with me. I believe what you and I did here with this book was God ordained. I will forever be grateful for your obedience to walk alongside me for this project. And thank you for bringing Jessica Johnson along to support me in this project.

Kat Armstrong—thank you for being relentless in resourcing me with the people needed to help me bring this project to life.

Mary DeMuth, my agent—thank you for believing in this book the minute you read my proposal.

To the team at Books & Such, especially Rachel Kent—thank you for your collective help with this project.

Deborah Gonzalez, my editor—I prayed for you. When you told me "This book was written for me," I knew you were the answer to my prayers for an editor who understood me and the point of this book.

To the entire team at NavPress—thank you for creating a community that embraces authors like me. I'm grateful to each of you.

Sharifa Stevens—thank you for being a sounding board whenever I needed your expertise.

Tricia Gordon—thank you for constantly reminding me to trust what the Spirit is doing.

To my sisters from around the world; the WU; my best friend from fifth grade, Anide Eustache; my ministry partner and friend, Betty Jean; the women of Haiti, Kenya, Uganda, Rwanda, the Democratic Republic of the Congo, Brazil, India, and the US— thank you. Thank you for teaching me about trauma and what each of you needed to heal. Thank you for being patient with me when my ego and fears would not allow me to fully see or understand your journey. Thank you for showing me love before you even knew me. Thank you for accepting me and elevating me so I can elevate others. And thank you for showing me beauty in the diversity of the sisterhood. This book is only possible because you each breathed life into me. So thank you.

Life is a journey

Top photo: Me and my sisters as kids, Haiti, circa 1977
Bottom photo: Me and my sisters all grown up,
New Jersey, 2019

Notes

CHAPTER 1 | BORN INTO TRAUMA

1. Edwidge Danticat, *The Farming of Bones* (New York: Soho Press, 1998), 224.

CHAPTER 2 | THE GOD WHO SEES YOU

1. Wilda C. Gafney, *Womanist Midrash: A Reintroduction to the Women of the Torah and the Throne* (Louisville, KY: Westminster John Knox Press, 2017), 41.

CHAPTER 3 | THE IMPACTS OF TRAUMA

1. *Diagnostic and Statistical Manual of Mental Disorders (DSM-5)*, 5th ed. (Washington, DC: American Psychiatric Association, 2013), 271.
2. "The Best Explanation of Addiction I've Ever Heard—Dr. Gabor Maté," November 16, 2020, https://www.youtube.com/watch?v=ys6TCO_olOc.
3. *Merriam-Webster Dictionary*, s.v. "heal," accessed July 14, 2023, https://www.merriam-webster.com/dictionary/heal.
4. Kristine P. Krafts, "Tissue Repair: The Hidden Drama," *Organogenesis* 6, no. 4 (October–December 2010): 225–33, https://www.ncbi.nlm.nih.gov/pmc/articles/PMC3055648.

CHAPTER 4 | "DO YOU WANT TO GET WELL?"

1. Henri Nouwen, "Jesus Is a Peacemaker," *Henry Nouwen Society* (blog), May 30, 2018, https://henrinouwen.org/meditations/jesus-is-a-peacemaker.

CHAPTER 5 | GRIEF

1. Elisabeth Kübler-Ross, *On Death and Dying: What the Dying Have to Teach Doctors, Nurses, Clergy, and Their Own Families* (New York: Scribner, 1997).

CHAPTER 6 | SHAME

1. Brené Brown, "Shame vs. Guilt," *Brené Brown* (blog), January 15, 2013, https://brenebrown.com/articles/2013/01/15/shame-v-guilt.
2. Brené Brown, "Shame Is Lethal," interview by Oprah Winfrey, March 24, 2013, https://www.youtube.com/watch?v=GEBjNv5M784.

CHAPTER 7 | DOMESTIC VIOLENCE

1. Angela N. Parker, *If God Still Breathes, Why Can't I? Black Lives Matter and Biblical Authority* (Grand Rapids: Eerdmans, 2021), 30.
2. Diane Langberg, *Redeeming Power: Understanding Authority and Abuse in the Church* (Grand Rapids: Brazos Press, 2020), 12–13.
3. Be sure to choose exercises appropriate to your condition and research proper form before engaging in new types of exercise.

CHAPTER 8 | SEXUAL ABUSE

1. "Statistics," National Sexual Violence Resource Center, accessed November 28, 2023, https://www.nsvrc.org/statistics.
2. "The Criminal Justice System: Statistics," Rape, Abuse & Incest National Network, accessed November 28, 2023, https://www.rainn.org/statistics /criminal-justice-system.
3. Phyllis Trible, *Texts of Terror: Literary-Feminist Readings of Biblical Narratives* (Philadelphia: Fortress Press, 1984), 38.
4. "Sexual Assault," RAINN, accessed July 18, 2023, https://www.rainn.org /articles/sexual-assault.
5. Phyllis Trible, "Ominous Beginnings for a Promise of Blessing," in *Hagar, Sarah, and Their Children: Jewish, Christian, and Muslim Perspectives*, ed. Phyllis Trible and Letty M. Russell (Louisville, KY: Westminster John Knox Press, 2006), 38.
6. Lisa Sharon Harper, *The Very Good Gospel: How Everything Wrong Can Be Made Right* (Colorado Springs: WaterBrook, 2016), 28.
7. Harper, *Very Good Gospel*, 29.
8. Maya Angelou. See *Rainbow in the Cloud: The Wisdom and Spirit of Maya Angelou* (New York: Random House, 2014), 51.

CHAPTER 9 | ABANDONMENT

1. Lindsay C. Gibson, *Adult Children of Emotionally Immature Parents: How to Heal from Distant, Rejecting, or Self-Involved Parents* (Oakland, CA: New Harbinger, 2015), 19–20.
2. Diane Poole Heller, "Attachment Styles," accessed July 21, 2023, https:// traumasolutions.com/attachment-styles-quiz. Heller's website—dianepoole heller.com—is a great resource for those who desire to go deeper. She even offers a free questionnaire and explanation of each attachment style. The quotes on the next two pages are from her.

3. See, for example, Brené Brown, *Daring Greatly: How the Courage to Be Vulnerable Transforms the Way We Live, Love, Parent, and Lead* (New York: Avery, 2015), 10.

CHAPTER 10 | RACIAL TRAUMA

1. Up through the Civil War era, the ownership and enslavement of Black bodies was the law of the land. But in spite of emancipation, Black people have experienced other forms of enslavement and oppression since then. The Reconstruction period of American history was marked by devastating public lynchings that created terror among Black people, a form of trauma for the victims and witnesses as well as for those who heard of it from a distance. Then there was the civil rights era, when Black people and their allies fought for Black people to merely exist and do basic things like sit, sleep, eat, and drink wherever they liked.

   In the modern day, racism and enslavement have taken a more covert form. Black people today are confronted with systemic racism at work, when dealing with government agencies and academic institutions, in society, and even at church. In other words, Black people in the US have suffered through hundreds of years of trauma without any concerted systematic effort to bring about public national biblical repentance, conciliation, and reparation.

2. Chanequa Walker-Barnes, *I Bring the Voices of My People: A Womanist Vision for Racial Reconciliation* (Grand Rapids: Eerdmans, 2019), 77.

3. Wilda C. Gafney, *Womanist Midrash: A Reintroduction to the Women of the Torah and the Throne* (Louisville, KY: Westminster John Knox Press, 2017), 42.

4. Christopher Connelly and Bobby Allyn, "Mourners Remember Atatiana Jefferson's 'Shining Smile' after Fort Worth Shooting," NPR, October 24, 2019, https://www.npr.org/2019/10/24/773193471/mourners-remember -atatiana-jeffersons-shining-smile-after-fort-worth-shooting.

5. "Father Dies Weeks after Daughter Is Shot and Killed by Texas Officer," November 10, 2019, CBS News, https://www.cbsnews.com/news/atatiana -jefferson-father-marquis-jefferson-dead-month-after-daughter-killed-by -police-officer-2019-11-10.

6. LaVendrick Smith, "Mother of Atatiana Jefferson, the Woman Slain by a Fort Worth Police Officer, Has Died," *Dallas Morning News*, January 9, 2020, https://www.dallasnews.com/news/2020/01/09/atatiana-jeffersons -mother-dies-according-to-family-attorney.

7. Frank Heinz, "Amber Carr, Sister of Atatiana Jefferson, Dies 'Surrounded by Family,' Attorney Says," NBC DFW, January 30, 2023, https://www .nbcdfw.com/news/local/amber-carr-sister-of-atatiana-jefferson-dies-at-33 -surrounded-by-family-attorney-says/3182058.

8. This book is not intended to address this form of trauma at length. There are great resources on the market that deal with this subject specifically.

9. Chichi Agorom, *The Enneagram for Black Liberation: Return to Who You Are beneath the Armor You Carry* (Minneapolis: Broadleaf Books, 2022), 9.

10. Agorom, *Enneagram for Black Liberation*, 11.

11. Resmaa Menakem, "Unlocking the Genius of Your Body," resmaa.com, December 18, 2020, https://www.resmaa.com/somatic-learnings/unlocking-the-genius-of-your-body.

12. Resmaa Menakem, *My Grandmother's Hands: Racialized Trauma and the Pathway to Mending Our Hearts and Bodies* (Las Vegas: Central Recovery Press, 2017), 35.

CHAPTER 12 | LAMENTING YOUR TRAUMA STORY

1. Soong-Chan Rah, *Prophetic Lament: A Call for Justice in Troubled Times* (Downers Grove, IL: InterVarsity Press, 2015), 21.

CHAPTER 13 | FORGIVING OTHERS

1. Peter Enns, *How the Bible Actually Works: In Which I Explain How an Ancient, Ambiguous, and Diverse Book Leads us to Wisdom Rather than Answers—and Why That's Great News* (New York: HarperOne, 2019), 31.

2. Enns, *How the Bible Actually Works*, 28–30.

3. Oprah Winfrey, *The Wisdom of Sundays: Life-Changing Insights from Super Soul Conversations* (New York: Flatiron Books, 2017), 110. On page 112 of Winfrey's book, "Forgiveness is giving up the hope that the past could have been any different" is attributed to Gerald G. Jampolsky, who appeared on *The Oprah Winfrey Show*.

4. Sharifa Stevens, "Wash Day, or Why I Love Unforgiveness," *When and Where I Enter* (blog), December 31, 2022, https://sharifahstevens.substack.com/p/wash-day.

5. Resmaa Menakem, "Unlocking the Genius of Your Body," resmaa.com, December 18, 2020, https://www.resmaa.com/somatic-learnings/unlocking-the-genius-of-your-body.

6. Thema Bryant-Davis, *Thriving in the Wake of Trauma: A Multicultural Guide* (Lanham, MD: AltaMira Press, 2008), 38.

CHAPTER 14 | FORGIVING YOURSELF

1. José Humphreys, sermon given at Metro Hope Church in Harlem, New York, February 12, 2023, https://www.youtube.com/watch?v=o27MrvTQ3Co.

2. Gustavo Gutiérrez, *Essential Writings*, ed. James B. Nickoloff (Minneapolis: Fortress Press, 1996), 192.

3. Adapted from "The Penitential Order: Rite Two," *The Book of Common Prayer* (New York: Church Publishing, 2007).

4. Numbers one through nine were modified from Lerner's "Nine Essential Ingredients of a True Apology" list found here: https://brenebrown.com/art/harriet-lerner-and-brene-im-sorry-how-to-apologize-why-it-matters. Harriet Lerner writes about this in *Why Won't You Apologize? Healing Big Betrayals and Everyday Hurts* (New York: Gallery Books, 2017).

5. Donnie McClurkin, "Stand," Sony/ATV Music, copyright © 1996.

CHAPTER 15 | REDISCOVERING HOPE

1. Christena Cleveland's article "The Privilege of Hopelessness" was posted in 2015 but is no longer accessible online.

2. Alice Walker, *The Color Purple* (Orlando: Harvest, 1982), 40.

3. These lyrics are occasionally included in the spiritual "Ain't Gonne Let Nobody Turn Me 'Round," although that's not where I encountered them.

4. Austin Channing Brown, *I'm Still Here: Black Dignity in a World Made for Whiteness* (New York: Convergent Books, 2018), 180.

CHAPTER 16 | EMBRACING JOY

1. Willie Jennings, "Joy and the Act of Resistance against Despair," interview by Miroslav Volf, *For the Life of the World* (podcast), episode 57, Yale Center for Faith & Culture, February 28, 2021. For interview transcript, see https://faith.yale.edu/media/joy-and-the-act-of-resistance-against-despair.

2. Jennings, "Joy and the Act of Resistance."

3. Wilda C. Gafney, *Womanist Midrash: A Reintroduction to the Women of the Torah and the Throne* (Louisville, KY: Westminster John Knox Press, 2017), 44.

4. Marianne Williamson, *A Return to Love: Reflections on the Principles of a Course in Miracles* (New York: HarperCollins, 1992), 191.

5. Jennings, "Joy and the Act of Resistance."

6. Alice Walker, quoted in Joseph Demakis, comp., *The Ultimate Book of Quotations* (Raleigh, NC: Lulu Enterprises, 2012), 170.

EPILOGUE

1. Wilda C. Gafney, *Womanist Midrash: A Reintroduction to the Women of the Torah and the Throne* (Louisville, KY: Westminster John Knox Press, 2017), 42.